Will there be Non-Christians in heaven?

A new edition with
The Meaning of Born Again

By
Jacques More

JAROM BOOKS

First published in Great Britain 2008

ISBN 978 1 898158 11 0

Published by *Jarom Books*
18 Rigby Close, Croydon, London
CR0 4JU – United Kingdom

www.jarom.net

Cover illustration by Sarah Rawlings
and Grange Graphics Ltd

Printed and bound by
CPI UK

To Opa

My Dutch grandfather who, as a Doctor
Helped at my birth and, in my rush
to enter the world
Is reputed to have been caught out still
smoking his cigar

CONTENTS

PREFACE

A mini bio

Jacques Robert More was born on the 11th of March 1958. The place of his birth is Tholen, a town south of the Netherlands. His mother also born in this town married a Frenchman and they lived in Paris. Whilst pregnant with Jacques, her father, the Doctor of Tholen, recommended he helped with the delivery. So this is how it was that Jacques came into the world in his grandparents' home. His parents divorced whilst he was very young. He then lived with his mum and two sisters, and in the summer of 1969, they moved to Kent, England, in the vicinity of Sevenoaks where Jacques has spent much of his life.

At the Wildernesse School in Sevenoaks, he first heard properly the gospel message that Jesus died for him and that He, was the One to turn to. So in 1972, at the age of 14, having had no religious upbringing or background, two evangelists, Justyn Rees and Max Sinclair carried out a school's outreach in the Sevenoaks area and the Friday night of that December week, Jacques gave his life to Jesus. At the age of 19 Jacques became a British Citizen.

Out of personal experiences during his first decade as a Christian, Jacques started to write in 1991 notes on the fruit/the evidence of deception in a group of believers, that is, 'What are the tell-tale signs?' (cf. his article *Wolf in Sheep's Clothing?* at www.jarom.net). Soon after, once the headline notes on the subject were written, he felt the Lord wanted him to put that work aside. He saw God's priority is to have 'The Real Thing' explained before 'The Counterfeit'. Not least is the need to speak into the present gaps in available Christian teaching which is how his first book arrived: *Will there be Non-Christians in heaven?*

This is a new edition of that book including *The meaning of born again* explaining the relevance of Jesus' words in John 3 relating to 'the righteous' who are also known as non-Christians.

About the Title

Will there be Non-Christians in Heaven? was not the original title. Probably the first that came to mind was *What happens to those who never hear the gospel?* This was thought a bit long-winded.

Then came *Can a Non-Christian be saved?* This one actually proved quite confusing.

I believe the gist of what is desired eventually came with *There will be Non-Christians in Heaven*, i.e. there will be some there along with the Christians.

This was probably too shocking, too strong for a first glance, so finally there was *Will there be Non-Christians in Heaven?*

I was originally reluctant to use the phrase 'get to heaven' or 'in heaven' because that actually implies this is a possible final place to be inhabited. By that I mean that in a belief in a heaven and a hell (which I hold) it could be thought that heaven is a final destination for some. Maybe I am being a bit pedantic, but I like to try and be accurate with what the Bible teaches. Allow me to explain very briefly. After all, this book is not intended as a book on unfulfilled prophecy.

Of the prophecies written in the Bible about the very final events in 'God's calendar', a new earth is mentioned which God will create (Isaiah 65:17 and 66:22, 2 Peter 3:13, Revelation 21:1). This new earth is then mentioned as the place where God will dwell (Revelation 21:3-4). Now if this is how it is going to be, and if I am one of His, I do not want to be in heaven forever whilst He is on this new earth with everyone else who belong to Him!

That was just to show why I was reluctant to originally use the phrase '. . . get to Heaven' or '. . . in Heaven' as part of the title. A more accurate understanding is '. . . as part of God's kingdom' or '. . . living in God's presence'.

What this Book is About

Principally this is a book about those who are generally known as non-Christians, who have never heard about Jesus and whom the Bible shows will be saved. That is to say this book is concerned with the biblical evidence for some non-Christians being accepted by God. For this, we will need a definition of a Christian and I do this in Chapter Two. I would first however like to lay a foundation.

Note

Due to the simplicity of reading, where Greek words are mentioned in this book the words are anglicised. So *hairesis* the Greek word for 'heresy' is how Greek words appear. Where a Greek word has one of the two Greek 'e's or one of the two 'o's I use the following: I have used an 'é' (an accented 'e') in place of the Greek letter *eta*; the other is *epsilon* = 'e'. Similarly 'o' is used for *omicron* and for *omega* therefore the accented 'ò' is used.

1

SOME GROUND RULES

Before we start properly I would like to lay a foundation, some ground rules, if you like. Indeed, from the outset it would be sensible to make clear the basis from which this book is written.

The Bible is the world's number 1 best seller and it is available in more languages than any other book (over 2000 to date). *Will there be Non-Christians in Heaven?* is written from the standpoint that this popular book, the Bible, is not like any other, but is Scripture. That is to say that the Bible is held by the author as inspired by God. It makes sense that if there is an omnipotent God who created all, then if He has also inspired the writings of the 66 books/letters contained in the Bible it is indeed a book worth considering.

This would also mean that there are no doctrinal contradictions within the whole of this assembly of writings known as the Bible. How could there logically be, if they are all inspired by such a God. So, the Bible is the ground, the foundation on which this book is written.

The Challenge

The challenge however really begins with its interpretation. What does the Bible actually teach? Indeed, it is possible to make the Bible say almost anything, even to the point of being able to declare that it says '***There is* no God**'. However, when you look at what is said in context it is a very different story:

> The fool has said in his heart, '*There is* no God.'
>
> *Psalm 14:1*

The above example is a simple one to show the effect of using a text taken out of context. Sometimes the context involves other chapters and other books contained in the Bible as the base needed to gain a balanced understanding.

Another aspect of reading the Bible which needs careful balancing is the reality that the truths contained within its pages are not always explicit but implicit. An example of this is the fact that 'God hates sin'. There is actually no explicit statement to this effect. What is shown is that there are many types of sin which He is seen as explicitly abhorrent about:

> These six *things* the LORD hates, yes, seven *are* an abomination to Him:
>
> A proud look, a lying tongue, hands that shed innocent blood, a heart that devises wicked plans, feet that are swift in running to evil, a false witness

> *who* speaks lies, and one who sows discord among brethren. *Proverbs 6:16-19*

So, it can be seen that 'God hates sin'. It is a truth which can be gained from the many implicit statements relating to it. The above passage was only one, but is already sufficient on its own to show the validity of the truth implied.

If an idea is held out of an implicit reading of a passage, it may then be true. But, if there is an explicit statement that is contrary to it somewhere else in the Bible, then it cannot be. Or, if there is another implied understanding elsewhere in scripture contrary to it, then it can only be held hypothetically, not as clear truth.

In conclusion of the above, what I am endeavouring to show is the possible dangers of reading into a passage what is not truth, as opposed to reading out of a passage what it can reveal.

The Berean Factor

In Greece there is an area known as Macedonia. In this region, west of the town of Thessaloniki (also known as Salonica), there used to be a town called Berea, now known as Véroia. The book of Acts found in the Bible contains a record of the travels of Paul the apostle and this includes the story of a trip he made to Berea.

Having preached in what was then known as Thessalonica, Paul journeyed west to Berea and spoke there to the Jews in their gathering place, the synagogue. Now they already had a portion of the Bible; the portion we now call the Old Testament. Paul himself was later to write about this part of the Bible to a fellow worker by the name of Timothy. This is what he wrote:

> All Scripture *is* given by inspiration of God, and *is* profitable for doctrine, for reproof, for correction, for instruction in righteousness, that the man of God may be complete, thoroughly equipped for every good work. *2 Timothy 3:16-17*

When Paul talked to the Bereans about what was to them new understandings from their Bible, they searched it, they studied it afresh, to see if what was said could indeed be understood in this 'new way'.

As a result many of them believed what Paul was saying. This is because their faith was already strong in the inspiration of Scripture. This faith was greater than that for their traditions and what they had been taught up till then. They were willing to change their previous standpoint because they were open to what was in the scriptures. The account of this can be found in Acts 17:10-12.

To be a follower of God and learn from Him like this is certainly worthwhile. That is, to be teachable yet not gullible, by learning for oneself out of the scripture what one has heard. A teacher of God's Word need never be afraid if his teaching is compared with any part of the Bible. If it is of God, founded upon what is true, the Bible will always confirm it. If not completely so, then the understanding he holds will need some reappraising.

As long as our attitude to one another is anything like the kind Paul recommended, we could learn a lot from each other.

> Brethren, if a man is overtaken in any trespass, you who *are* spiritual restore such a one in a spirit of gentleness, considering yourself lest you also be tempted. *Galatians 6:1*

A clear emphasis is placed here on this being done in a spirit of gentleness.

A Spiritual Book

Another very important point to consider is that if understanding the Bible was just an intellectual exercise, just as with a scientific book, there would be few differences between interpretations. This is not so.

Since the Bible is inspired by God and God is a Spirit, it follows that the Bible is a spiritual book. Jesus said of God,

> God *is* Spirit, and those who worship Him must worship in spirit and truth. *John 4:24*

A passage of the Bible may be read often and one day a whole new understanding, a whole new meaning, is gained from this old familiar text. This is the property, the facet of this book I call spiritual. The Holy Spirit can open up the reader's mind, his understanding about a passage, in a way no one else can. Jesus spoke of the Holy Spirit to his disciples prior to leaving them when he said:

> I still have many things to say to you, but you cannot bear *them* now. However, when He, the Spirit of truth, has come, He will guide you into all truth . . .
>
> *John 16:12-13*

Paul writing to the Christians in Corinth, now known as Korinthos in Greece, explained a bit about this,

> These things we also speak, not in words which man's wisdom teaches but which the Holy Spirit teaches, comparing spiritual things with spiritual. But the natural man does not receive the things of the Spirit of God, for they are foolishness to him; nor can he know *them*, because they are spiritually discerned. *1 Corinthians 2:13-14*

What Jesus was saying to his disciples was that there were new things which they would learn, after he was eventually to depart from them. Not unlike the way the Bereans learned new things from their Bible when Paul came to see them. One example with the disciples is the way that they learned about salvation and the gift of the Holy Spirit, as something also to be offered to the Gentiles: the non-Jews. The account of this is in Acts 10:1 on to 11:18.

Up until that time their understanding was not fruitful as to what the Bible was saying concerning the Gentiles. But, after that, they were able to see new things. They had gained this knowledge, this insight by the Holy Spirit's guidance through others. Up till then this truth was only spiritually discerned as Paul puts it. Paul himself had gained this understanding about the Gentiles having a place in God's heart. It was revealed to him even before Peter was put in a position to lead the church in gaining this truth. See the accounts of Paul's conversion before Peter himself was taught these same truths (Acts 9:1-19, 26:12-18, etc.).

A man named Simeon was also aware of this truth before the early disciples generally understood it. He knew that Jesus would be for salvation of all peoples, including the Gentiles. This was revealed to him by the Spirit (Luke 2:25-35). This is what Simeon said in thanks to God when he took Jesus as a baby in his arms:

> Lord, now . . . my eyes have seen Your salvation which You have prepared before the face of all peoples, a light to *bring* revelation to the Gentiles, and the glory of Your people Israel. *Luke 2:29-32*

This helps to show that asking God's help to understand as you read the Bible is the fastest way to learn what it contains. With a Spiritual angle in mind it is also important to be aware of where bad teaching comes from. The Bible speaks clearly about an enemy of God and of Mankind: the Devil and all those with him. It is possible as believers to take hold of what this enemy teaches for ourselves; usually because it is attractive at its inception.

> Now the Spirit expressly says that in latter times some will depart from the faith, giving heed to deceiving spirits and doctrines of demons . . . *1 Timothy 4:1*

The capital 'S' of Spirit is there to show Paul is here talking about the Holy Spirit. The mention is made of people who depart from the faith. So that it becomes clear that the Holy Spirit says believers, people in the faith, are able to depart from the faith by listening and taking on board what has been presented to them by the enemy: the Devil and his minions. When it says depart from the faith it is talking, as in the context, of deviating from sound teaching and doctrine.

This serves to make clear that the originators and the source of false teaching is the enemy. It also shows that any believer has the capacity for listening to what the enemy teaches. Just as the Holy Spirit can 'open eyes' to scripture, the Devil can 'veil eyes' so a meaning is hidden (2 Corinthians 4:3-4).

The teaching that is false, that deviates from sound doctrine, is known as heresy. This heresy, this bad teaching, is not always just a matter of interpretations of the Bible out of context, like the simple example above which inferred '***There is* no God**'. This particular type could be thought of as good food with bits taken out, thus making it incomplete or unbalanced. Eaten too regularly this food will definitely inhibit a healthy growth.

The other way food can be made harmful is when something bad is added from another source. Like an omelette which is being prepared and then another egg is added which proves to be rotten; it is tainted by its poisoning effects. This makes the whole omelette unfit for consumption. Jesus used a similar illustration with leaven, which is another word for yeast. Yeast is a most common type of leaven. He is talking about something being added to an existing mix. This is what Jesus said:

> . . . Take heed and beware of the leaven of the Pharisees and the Sadducees . . . *Matthew 16:6*

The disciples who Jesus was teaching were not really sure of what he was saying. They wondered if it was because of the fact that they had forgotten to bring some bread with them. Noticing this Jesus replied:

> 'How is it you do not understand that I did not speak to you concerning bread? – *but* you should beware of the leaven of the Pharisees and Sadducees.'
>
> Then they understood that He did not tell *them* to beware of the leaven of bread, but of the doctrine of the Pharisees and Sadducees. *Matthew 16:11-12*

The Pharisees and Sadducees were particular religious groups of Jesus' day. He was telling his disciples to beware of their teaching. If they were not careful with some of what was taught by these two groups of people, it would influence everything else they believed, and prove harmful. Adding this kind of teaching would take away from the quality of what they already had. It would permeate and influence it all badly.

So, taking something out of what God says gives a bad teaching, i.e. 'A text out of context is a pretext', and, adding something to what God said also can give a bad teaching, i.e. 'The bad omelette' idea. Not forgetting of course, who is the actual originator of these additions and the inspiration behind believing half-truths: veiling the eyes to the other half.

Pharisees and Sadducees

An example of the omelette idea in the Bible is the teaching of the Pharisees concerning the Sabbath. The Sabbath, a Saturday, was declared special by God as a day set aside for rest from work of the previous 6 days.

> Remember the Sabbath day, to keep it holy. Six days you shall labour and do all your work, but the seventh day *is* the Sabbath of the LORD your God. *In it* you shall do no work: you, nor your son, nor your daughter, nor your manservant, nor your maidservant, nor your cattle, nor your stranger who

> *is* within your gates. For *in* six days the LORD made the heavens and the earth, the sea, and all that *is* in them, and rested the seventh day. Therefore the LORD blessed the Sabbath day and hallowed it.
>
> *Exodus 20:8-11*

This command of God was given through Moses in about the 15th century BC to the people of Israel. It was a revolutionary and compassionate decree when compared with how the nations lived in those days, with much slavery and abuse of people. The thought of a day of rest in seven for yourself, any slave, and any working animal was a concept 'out of this world'.

Now the Pharisees had lots of good points about them. They believed in the inspiration of Scripture, they saw the importance of learning what God's Word said, etc.

However, in their interpretation of it, in their practice, they added so much to what it said. They added extra rules which God never gave, so that (in their minds), God's will could be satisfied.

The gist of the original command was to give a day of rest in seven, just as God originally used it. The Pharisees added to this, particular ways in which your time could and could not be used on such a day. So much so that when someone needed to be healed, far be it, that this was to be done on a Sabbath. That was work!

Jesus had several encounters with the Pharisees on the Sabbath. This is one of them.

> And behold, there was a man who had a withered hand. And they asked Him, [the Pharisees asked Jesus] saying, 'Is it lawful to heal on the Sabbath?' – that they might accuse Him. Then He said to them, 'What man is there among you who has one sheep, and if it falls into a pit on the Sabbath, will not lay hold of it and lift *it* out? Of how much more value then is a man than a sheep? Therefore it is lawful to do good on the Sabbath.' Then He said to the man, 'Stretch out your hand'. And he stretched *it* out, and it was restored as whole as the other. *Matthew 12:10-13*

On another occasion with the Pharisees Jesus said:

> . . . The Sabbath was made for man, and not man for the Sabbath. *Mark 2:27*

So this gives us a good example of the value of what God had said being diminished by an addition applied to it, by the extra rules applied to this Day of rest.

Unlike the Pharisees, the Sadducees did not have much faith in what was written in the Scripture. They found it hard to believe in a resurrection of the dead and anything miraculous. They were not unlike today's liberal thinkers within Christendom.

Heresy

Looking at heresy a bit further, it is interesting to take a glance at a letter Paul wrote to a group of Christians in another region known as Galatia, which is now an area of Turkey.

Paul's letters make up a significant part of the New Testament section of the Bible. They are equally referred to as books and the dividing up of these writings into chapters and verses occurred much later. The chapters were put in during the 13th century by Stephen Langdon, Archbishop of Canterbury, possibly whilst in exile in Paris. Also in Paris but in 1551, verses were first included by a Bible publisher called Robert Stephanus (though he may have done this whilst in Geneva). All these divisions are useful, as aids to enable pointing exactly to a place quoted.

In chapter 5 of his letter to the Galatians, Paul makes a list of what he terms 'works of the flesh' i.e. the kind of produce a life of carnal desire exhibits: The acts or doings of the wrong inclinations of human nature.

> Now the works of the flesh are evident, which are: adultery, fornication, uncleanness, licentiousness, idolatry, sorcery, hatred, contentions, jealousies, outbursts of wrath, selfish ambitions, dissensions, heresies, envy, murders, drunkenness, revelries, and the like; of which I tell you beforehand, just as I also told *you* in time past, that those who practise such things will not inherit the kingdom of God.
>
> *Galatians 5:19-21*

What I wish to bring out of this passage is that heresy which is a part of the list is therefore a work of the flesh.

The Greek word is *hairesis*. There is actually no other Greek word to translate the English 'heresy'.

The Greek word itself has been translated otherwise as 'factions', 'sects', etc. It comes from *haireomai* and I quote from Strong's Greek dictionary of the New Testament showing that this is, '. . . to take for oneself, i.e. to prefer:- choose . . .'. Concerning *hairesis* Strong's has '. . . prop. a choice, i.e. (spec.) a party or (abstr.) disunion:- heresy [which is the Gr. word itself], sect' (Strong's Concordance and lexicon: Copyright 1890 by James Strong Madison, N.J.).

This all serves to help show that although the originator of bad teaching is the enemy, a choice for this teaching – a decision to believe it – is made at some point: First, it is a move towards it, a leaning then, it is chosen. A false teaching is attractive to the flesh because it usually engenders self importance and pride. The attractions to the flesh include that one has the right teaching, we are the first, (i.e. others are excluded), etc.

So, basically by the above it can be seen that heresy is a choice.

Once a choice is made to believe the teaching however, a door to hear otherwise is often closed. The latch, the handle to open this door is always on the inside. I am talking about a kind of door in one's mind and heart, closed to any teaching contrary to what one has chosen to believe.

The idea is not new that a Christian can have a door closed, thus shutting God out and what He wants. This is why, *when speaking to Christians* Jesus said:

> Behold, I stand at the door and knock. If anyone hears My voice and opens the door, I will come in to him and dine with him, and he with Me.
>
> *Revelation 3:20*

A door of the life of Christians can be shut such that Jesus would like to come in. There is a need then to recognise when Jesus is outside knocking on the door. In the same overall passage (Revelation 3:14-22) Jesus counselled these same Christians to,

> . . . anoint your eyes with eye salve, that you may see.
>
> *Revelation 3:18*

This shows us that a Christian can have his view restricted from seeing what Jesus wants him to see. Notice that in both cases, it is the individual's responsibility to open the door or anoint their own eyes.

But, if they can't see already, how can they know that they need to see? On their own they cannot!

This is why it's important to keep an open mind with reference to the Scripture, just like the Bereans, in particular when someone brings something which has not been heard that way before, or at all.

The wonderful thing is that God cares about His people so much that He regularly sends a witness to the truth. Just like the prophets of old He sent regularly to the people of Israel. The difficulties arise when those whom God sends are marginalised, isolated and excluded. Jesus said this would happen (John 16:2).

So when God sends someone across our path to speak to us as He does often, let us listen and check it out. This is similar to another of Paul's instructions, this time to the Christians back in Thessalonica

> Do not quench the Spirit. Do not despise prophecies. Test all things; hold fast what is good.
>
> *1 Thessalonians 5:19-21*

Paul also said,

> Therefore let him who thinks he stands take heed lest he fall. *1 Corinthians 10:12*

I am emphasising all this because it is so important. Paul certainly thought so. To show how greatly Paul valued the understanding of the dangers and harm caused by deception this is some of what he said at his last meeting with the leaders of the church at Ephesus:

> . . . take heed to yourselves and to all the flock, among which the Holy Spirit has made you overseers, to shepherd the church of God which He purchased with His own blood. For I know this, that after my departure savage wolves will come in among you, not sparing the flock. Also from among yourselves men will rise up, speaking perverse things, to draw away the disciples after themselves. Therefore watch . . . *Acts 20:28-31*

This he said clearly to the elders of the church, that among themselves, the very elders, men will rise up speaking perverse things, etc. We know this was specifically said to the leaders because Paul had called the elders to him so he could speak with them face to face (see verse 17).

The challenge is, whether you are a leader or not, as a believer the possibility is there to be drawn away from the truth. One possible way this state of affairs could be looked at is that it is one of God's methods to show us how much we need each other. Just as Peter and the rest of the Jews with him needed Paul at one time; to challenge them and help them see where they were going astray. See Galatians 2:11-16 and Paul's advice as mentioned above in Galatians 6:1.

Nothing would please me more than to know that at as you read this book you emulate the Bereans by arming yourself with a Bible, 'find out if these things are so' (Acts 17:11) and talk to God asking Him to open up His Word to you.

2

AN INTRODUCTION

The word 'Christian' has been with us for nearly 2000 years. The original meaning has changed to mean different things to different people. It would therefore be useful at the very beginning to give a definition of 'a Christian' in order to enter into a meaningful discussion.

The definition thought of I present as a sentence often spoken by keen Christians in their efforts to share the Good News of Salvation (that is, 'the gospel'). It is in fact their view of how one becomes a Christian:

Unless you come to know the Lord Jesus Christ (consciously) as your saviour whilst you are alive, you will not be saved.

This is then often supported by the verse in John's Gospel where Jesus says,

> . . . I am the way, the truth, and the life. No one comes to the Father except through Me. *John 14:6*

Now, if this is how one becomes a Christian and what was truly meant by this verse, indeed if this is the whole truth as gained from it, then what happens to:

- The man born deaf and blind – is he held accountable for not hearing the gospel?
- The man who dies at a young age, before his reasoning ability and decision-making facilities are developed – is he destined to hell?
- The man born in a remote – or even – in a populated area, who never hears the gospel – is he forbidden to enter the Kingdom of God?

Now God is Just and will do what is right (Genesis 18:25). However, is this enough theology (understanding of God), enough teaching to explain what happens to those who die without the knowledge of Jesus?

More substance than that is needed to prevent the possible condemnation of so many in our minds. This, in itself, would lead to inability to relate with such folk in many areas, thus weakening effectiveness as witnesses to the gospel of the Kingdom.

Indeed, if this is all, that John 14:6 can mean (as in the 'definition' above), then all the above categorised people will go to hell. Since not being saved means that is where one ends up!

However, the above verse clearly understood in this way, does not explain or make it easy to see why some people are known as righteous by God without their ever hearing the name of the Lord Jesus Christ. This is, of course, immediately assuming that God does hold some people as righteous outside of this particular knowledge.

Well, does He?

In Hebrews 11:4 we read that Abel, Adam's second son, was held as righteous before God. Clearly, this is someone who is thought as being worthy by some way of salvation and, therefore, not going to be found in hell. This being so, then already, the original meaning given of John 14:6 in the beginning of this discussion cannot be totally correct.

Are there any other people whom we can clearly see as held righteous by God without their being aware of the name of the Lord Jesus Christ?

Yes, in Genesis 5:21-24 we read of a man named Enoch. He is a man recognised as never having died – for God took him. A man again held as righteous before God; indeed, Hebrews 11:5 tells us that he was pleasing to God. However, we have no record of either Abel or Enoch having any knowledge of the Lord Jesus. Remember this is talking of a conscious knowledge.

We could go on to speak of men such as Abraham, Moses, Elijah, Daniel, etc. men who are on record as being God's men and His being pleased with them. However, there is no record of their having personal knowledge of the Lord Jesus Christ as their Saviour, as understood by the flavour of the 'definition' at the start of this discussion. But, are these not men of faith, men who knew God, who had a relationship with Him?

Yes, but there is no suggestion or record that they knew the Lord Jesus Christ by name in their life on earth.

Now, you may already question my argument as being limited so far to Old Testament characters. You may after all, view God as dealing with people differently in different time periods. This is a view, an understanding which comes out of 'Dispensation' thinking. This is the idea that God is believed to treat people differently according to when they lived ('dispensing' different judgments according to time). Does the Bible teach this?

3

DISPENSATIONS

Having spoken only of Old Testament individuals so far, as acceptable to God, it would be reasonable to look at this idea of dispensations. Dividing up different periods of time in this way would say that we are in a different dispensation now, than the aforementioned individuals.

That is to say, we are in an age, a time period, in which God deals with men differently than the way He did then. For example, the idea that in Old Testament times, and before Jesus came on the scene, God 'dispensed' a different view (or judgment) of men than after Jesus and His gospel had begun to be preached.

If this is valid, then the examples above of Old Testament characters cannot give also a valid testimony on how God treats people today. But, if dispensational thinking like this is a view without foundation in scripture, then the examples given so far are very much of value in an understanding of how God treats modern man. It would be wise then to look at this idea.

The overall idea of dispensations of time involves grouping various periods of God's Revelation or Dealings with Man into sections historically, spaced in intervals by a particular event. An example of this is an interval based on a 'Judgment' by God, as can be seen by way of Figure 1.

The events here are slotted into seven different time periods of unequal lengths. Although it is arguable that all the events mentioned at the divisions are accurately termed 'Judgments' (in the sense that they are all a punishment, a retribution), the setting out of sections of events within Scripture in this manner is a very good aid to memorising and learning. It is a great help to picture events as part of a whole by use of different time periods or slots.

To then translate this idea (of dispensations), into a meaning that God treats people differently in these different time slots is, however, to stray from the revealed evidence in the Bible. There would need to be explicit reference of God doing this. Instead we find the opposite.

What we find is a treatment of individuals, not according to when they lived, but according to what they knew in their lifetime and what they did with it: A judgment directly in proportion to the revealed Truths of God, Right and Wrong, etc., as put into practise.

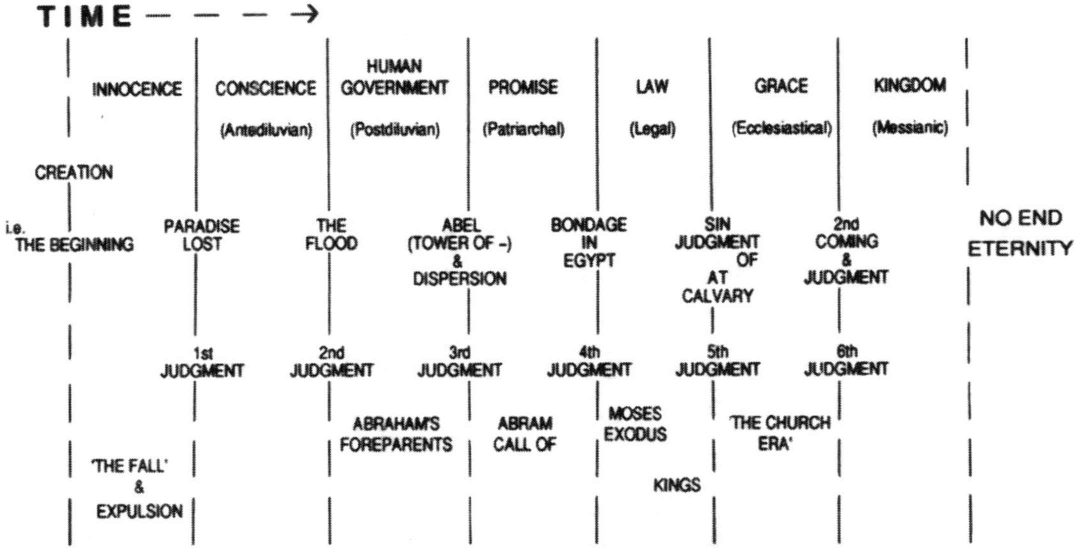

This diagram is based upon information taken from THE NEW PANORAMA BIBLE STUDY COURSE by A. E. EADE with the permission of Kingsway Publications, Eastbourne.

Figure 1 – An example of Dispensations of Time.

> For there is no partiality with God [as to who and when]. For as many as have sinned without law will also perish without law [i.e. without knowledge of God and particular Rights and Wrongs], and as many as have sinned in the law will be judged by the law . . . for not the hearers of the law *are* just in the sight of God, but the doers of the law will be justified . . . *Romans 2:11-13*

This passage categorically tells us that judgment is appropriated in accordance to what was known when one sins. It is in direct regard to the revelation of truth obtained. Dispensation thinking then, is therefore mainly of value in the realm of teaching aids. To stray into applying the idea of dispensations to explain salvation's application in categorical cut off time points in this or any way would thus be erroneous.

A better way to view the biblical perspective, I think, would be as in Figure 2.

In this diagram, we see that there is one cut-off point where all mankind on earth was destroyed by the Flood, with the exception of Noah and his immediate family ('the 8' who were saved). Judgment is applied no differently to individuals within the two realms of time shown. The schematic diagram, however, shows clear distinction between groups of people according to Revelation; according to where the knowledge imparted differ.

A more general 'feeling' for dispensations involves the thinking that there is a distinct difference

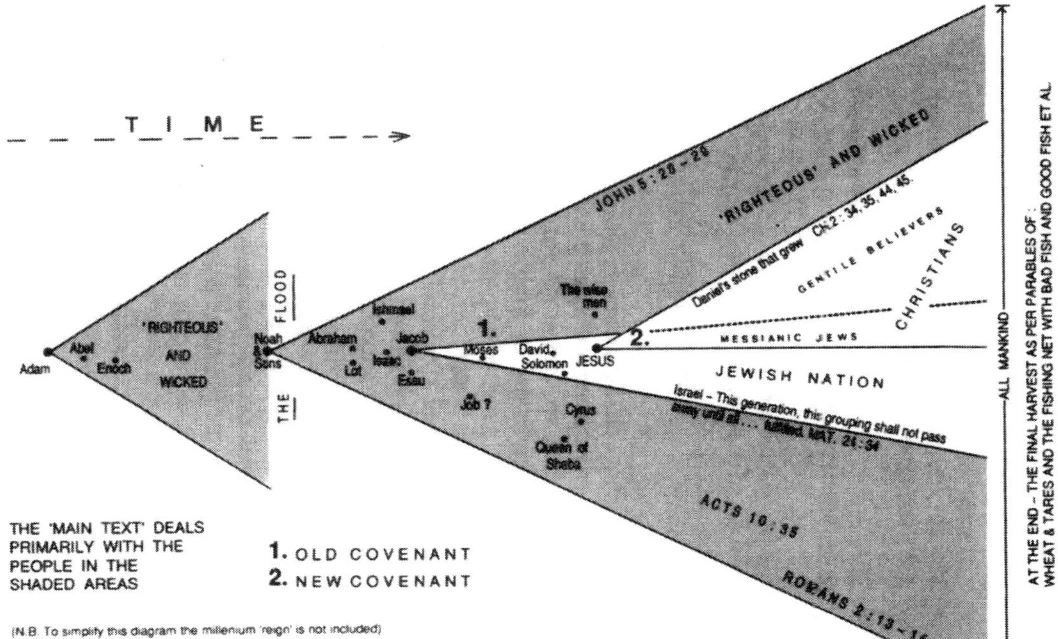

Figure 2 – The Biblical Perspective

with people in relation to God before Christ as opposed to after Christ. There is a real sense in which the relationship aspect is dissimilar. Before Jesus came, there was an incomplete revelation of God and His ways. Also, knowing Jesus personally as one's Lord and being empowered by the Holy Spirit, was never previously a 'free for all' (the empowering). This applies clearly, however, to all those to whom it is presented, not in a cut-off time point. What about those who had not received such news, i.e. those who live in the same time period?

Long after Jesus returned to heaven, whole Jewish families scattered abroad had not yet even heard of His coming, let alone of salvation through Him. So, it is clear, that there are no time cut-off points. There is a cut-off distinction only according to the degree of Revelation or knowledge known. The same is true of people who even today have never heard. Each person is judged according to Revealed Truth that they know and what they do with it. Ask yourself this question: 'Does God really treat people according to when they lived, with particular time cut-off points, i.e. which of the two diagrams depict a more honest view as to how God deals with people as shown by the Bible?'

The Three Groups in Figure 2

Let us consider the three main groups of people/ categories of revealed truth imparted briefly, as show in Figure 2.

The 'last' involves those of the Christian Faith of whom Paul wrote,

> . . . if you confess with your mouth the Lord Jesus and believe in your heart that God has raised Him from the dead, you will be saved. *Romans 10:9*

So no problem here

The second, is the Jewish grouping 'Israel'. A man born a Jew, full of faith and diligence in being a Jew in regards to 'The Law', is acknowledged as having salvation by Jesus, for when he is asked what is to be done to inherit eternal life, he says, '**Keep the commandments**', and clearly approves of this fulfilment being the prerequisite of the inheritance of eternal life in this situation.

> Now behold, one came and said to Him, 'Good Teacher, what good thing shall I do that I may have eternal life?' So He said to him, '. . . if you want to enter into life, keep the commandments.'
>
> *Matthew 19:16-17*
>
> *Also Mark 10:17-19 & Luke 18:18-20*

Jesus clearly did not add to this requirement in this clear context. So a Jew, not having heard the message of the Christian gospel, but fully believing and practising the Law of Moses, will be saved.

Let us now look at the remaining category and in particular 'The Righteous' among them.

'The Wicked' I do not discuss in detail here but in chapter 9. Basically, if they remain in a state of practising evil, they do not have peace and are destined for everlasting punishment. See Isaiah 57:20-21, Matthew 25:46 et al.

A man born a Gentile (that is, a non-Jew) does not have the Law of Moses; if, also, he does not hear the Gospel of Jesus how is he judged?

> . . . not the hearers of the law *are* just in the sight of God, but the doers of the law will be justified; for when Gentiles, who do not have the law, by nature do the things *contained* in the law, these, although not having the law, are a law to themselves, who show the work of the law written in their hearts . . .
>
> *Romans 2:13-15*

He is judged against what he knows to be right and wrong – what is actually revealed and manifested to him; according to the 'law written in his heart' as in the verses above.

So if he, against conscience, practises evil, he is rightfully condemned.

But, if he follows what is right, within his capacity of knowledge and understanding, then he is acceptable, not out of the deeds he has or has not done, but out of the purpose, the intent of heart (the faith) which led him to carry out those deeds. The deeds are only the fruit. They are evidence of the state of heart, out of the 'nature' of the heart in which 'the work of the law' is written. Whether it is either a heart of faith, believing and thus active in 'good works of righteousness', or, a heart of unbelief (in these things), thus quenching conscience, succumbing to 'flesh's weakness', practising evil. This is expanded upon in later chapters.

Does he come to the Light or does he shun it and turn to Darkness?

> For everyone practising evil hates the light and does not come to the light, lest his deeds should be exposed. *John 3:20*

What light? Jesus, who is

> . . . the true Light which gives light to every man who comes into the world. *John 1:9*

So that, the condemnation of such is (i.e. for the wicked),

> . . . that the light has come into the world, and men [of such kind] loved darkness rather than light, because their deeds were evil. *John 3:19*

Freedom to choose, ability to change his mind, is never taken from Man, so anyone in 'any category' who decides to practise evil is in danger.

Is there a Gentile who had not heard the Gospel, shown to us in the Bible, as approved by God? Indeed, does the 'Christian Era' show up in the Bible people who are acceptable to God outside of knowing the Lord Jesus Christ as their Saviour and Lord?

I believe the classic example is that of Cornelius, the Roman (Gentile) Centurion and all those like him who, as recorded in the book of Acts are spoken of by Peter, when he says,

> . . . In truth I perceive that God shows no partiality. But in every nation [in every race] whoever fears Him and works righteousness is accepted by Him.
>
> *Acts 10:34-35*

This he said before he spoke about Jesus to Cornelius and his companions. That is to say, we have a record in the New Testament of God accepting men who have no knowledge of His son Jesus Christ but who are seen to fear Him by the righteous deeds that they perform. They are looked at with due regards to their deeds, as a natural outworking of an inward faith in those kind of things being right (their deeds).

> . . . for when Gentiles [non-Jews and therefore non-recipients of the law, and also, all non-recipients of the Gospel of Jesus Christ] who do not have the law, by nature do the things *contained* in the law, these, although not having the law, are a law to themselves . . . *Romans 2:14*

> . . . for not the hearers of the law *are* just in the sight of God, but the doers of the law will be justified . . .
>
> *Romans 2:13*

As mentioned, please see following chapters for a fuller understanding behind this.

Other Dispensation Issues

Another problem with the idea of Dispensations is to make God appear different (or to act different) in Old Testament times as compared with the New, let alone the subtle questioning as to the relevance of the Old Testament today. This goes against New Testament references such as 2 Timothy 3:16.

> All Scripture *is* given by inspiration of God, and *is* profitable for doctrine, for reproof, for correction, for instruction in righteousness, that the man of God may be complete, thoroughly equipped for every good work. *2 Timothy 3:16-17*

Paul is here writing about the Old Testament. We also have verses telling us that the Old Testament was written for examples to the Christians, clearly showing God's unchanging nature and behaviour towards men, e.g. in 1 Corinthians 10:11 (and context) we read,

> Now all these things happened to them [to the Israelites in the wilderness] as examples, and they were written for our admonition . . .
> *1 Corinthians 10:11*

This clearly shows God's judgment in the Old Testament as a relevant testimony to the readers of the New.

Oh, how true, therefore in the context of his dealings with men, is God's own statement in Malachi:

> . . . I *am* the LORD, I do not change . . . *Malachi 3:6*

There is also the statement in Hebrews 13:8 about Jesus Christ being the same yesterday, today and forever.

An Apostolic Age

One further area of belief which comes out of 'Dispensation thinking', is that of an apostolic age existing up to the death of the first 'Twelve', which is now therefore over. This serves to back up the idea that the age of miracles done through God's servants is over, that is, in the same manner as done by the 'first' apostles.

Looked at more closely, we find however that the apostles mentioned in the New Testament are not restricted to the twelve, and apostles have continued to be chosen, called out, well after the Resurrection and Ascension of the Lord Jesus.

When Judas Iscariot died, a '13th' apostle was appointed to take his place, Matthias in Acts 1:26.

Then we see Saul of Tarsus, a '14th' apostle, better known as Paul (Romans 1:1). When mentioning in his writings the various ministries which were active in the Church at large, Paul lists apostles, prophets, evangelists, and pastors and teachers (Ephesians 4:11).

I do not know anyone seriously suggesting evangelists and pastors and teachers being no longer relevant. So why reject the relevancy of apostles today (or even prophets)?

The Greek word for 'apostle' just means 'sent out', so an apostle is someone called out, especially chosen or picked and sent out. To this end, we can see Barnabas as an apostle as shown by,

> . . . the Holy Spirit said, 'Now separate to Me Barnabas and Saul for the work to which I have called them'. *Acts 13:2*

Barnabas would then be a '15th' apostle.

However, these are still just a few clear examples of apostles other than the 'Twelve'. What we do have, to further show the continuing relevance of the 'office' is definite implication of its existence in general. For example, in the last book of the Bible, Revelation, we read of the Lord Jesus Christ saying to the church at Ephesus,

> . . . you have tested those who say they are apostles and are not . . . *Revelation 2:2*

Paul, in writing to the church at Corinth said,

> . . . such *are* false apostles, deceitful workers . . .
> *2 Corinthians 11:13*

These passages reveal clearly the existence of false apostles: counterfeits of those with the real office or function of apostleship. This clearly implies that others – true apostles – were about beyond the 'original' few.

Also, if the number of apostles God used was limited to a dozen or more, it would not have been too difficult to learn all their names by heart. The list of the twelve as is found in the gospels could be circulated, i.e. Luke 6:12-16. There would therefore be no difficulty in spotting any false ones.

It can therefore be seen that indeed the ministry of apostles is relevant today.

Miracles

As far as miracles are concerned and the apostles being the 'only' ones to do them, Jesus commanded His disciples (that is, the apostles) to make disciples of all the nations . . .

> . . . teaching them to observe all things that I have commanded you . . . *Matthew 28:19-20*

One of these commands as shown earlier in that same gospel is to,

> Heal the sick . . . *Matthew 10:8*

And the attitude, the manner in which this was to be done, Jesus explained by the phrase 'Freely you have received, freely give' (Matthew 10:8).

We also read in Luke 10 that the Lord sent out 70 others to heal. Therefore, healing, etc. is not an exclusive function of apostles.

Just like Philip whom we know as an evangelist did miracles (Acts 8:6), And, Stephen the 'deacon' in Acts 6, who,

> . . . did great wonders and signs among the people.
> *Acts 6:8*

4

AN UNDERSTANDING

Having seen what happened to Abel, Enoch, Moses, Elijah and other Old Testament Characters can be a relevant testimony to how God treats people today, let us continue with them.

As far as the above men are concerned, there seems to be a broad consensus that they will not be found in hell; they will be saved: they will be in the presence of the Father. This being so, what other meaning can we gain of John 14:6, in particular where it says,

> . . . No one comes to the Father except through Me.

As we can see, the above named are persons and, with little disaccord, they are men who will be or who are in the presence of the Father. This then truly shows the need to move away from the particular understanding of the verse, that one must know (consciously) the Lord Jesus Christ in one's life on earth as one's own saviour, in order to be saved (as it's sole meaning), i.e. for everybody.

What is a possible alternative meaning?

For a clear answer, one that is a positive reply, I believe it would be useful to see this topic in a fuller context. It will be helpful to go back to the first mention of salvation, that is to say, to the first chapters of Genesis: The first place where a need for salvation can be seen.

Adam and Eve

In Genesis 2 and 3 we see sin enter the lives of Adam and Eve for the first time when they went against God by disobeying His command. Now, for as much as they went along with their new-found sinful nature with which they had clothed themselves, they then became slaves to sin.

> Do you not know that to whom you present yourselves slaves to obey, you are that one's slaves whom you obey, whether of sin to death, or of obedience to righteousness? *Romans 6:16*

Already in Genesis Chapter 3, three pages or so into the beginning of the Bible we can see a need for salvation: A need to be saved from sin and its effect. God then intervened with various statements as well as promises; indeed, He made some very strong pronouncements (Genesis 3:1-21).

The two particularly relevant to this current topic which I wish to mention involve, first, a verbal declaration and second, a non-verbal declaration in the form of an illustration. They are:

(1) A ruling upon the serpent (Genesis 3:14-15). (The serpent is also known as the Devil and Satan – see Revelation 12:9). He had deceived the woman (later known as Eve, see Genesis 3:20), into eating the forbidden fruit.

    God said He would cause the woman's Seed to bruise the serpent's head.

(2) An action of God's (Genesis 3:21). He made coats (or tunics) of skin to clothe Adam and Eve.

These were big and meaningful statements. In both the above declarations, God showed that He was the prime mover, the instigator. He declared himself as the person to bring this about.

First, He would cause the woman's Seed – the person born by woman alone, to be the one to remove Satan's power (by bruising his head). This person is no other than Jesus Christ himself. He is the only one on biblical record to be born of a virgin (Isaiah 7:14, Matthew 1:23 et al.). Born without the germination of a man's seed, hence the title, 'The woman's Seed'.

The second act mentioned involved God killing animals. He then removed their skins, and clothed Adam and Eve with the skins. Some versions have it as skin, some as skins. I shall use the plural for ease of communication of the thoughts around this matter.

There is of course a very practical benefit in God doing this. Once they had recognised that they were naked, Adam and Eve had sewn fig leaves together and made coverings with these (Genesis 3:7). Fig leaves would not last long as items of clothing, and thus, a better and more hardwearing material (skins of animals, i.e. leather) was provided for them by God: A practical sign of God's care and provision.

The meaning of God's actions however, they go much deeper than just providing a better material, for items of physical clothing. First, God had to kill some animals. He is therefore on record as being the first person to shed blood and kill. This alone is very significant, because God's first mention of death (the first in the Bible) was originally to Adam:

> . . . Of every tree of the garden you may freely eat; but of the tree of the knowledge of good and evil you shall not eat, for in the day that you eat of it you shall surely die. [Lit. dying you shall die]
>
> *Genesis 2:16-17*

God talked of death to Adam; to His own image. He mentioned how Adam's own death was a reality to be grasped in the event of his eating the forbidden fruit. The tree this fruit belonged to was in the garden with other trees which Adam could eat from. We need to picture what this is like.

You have to put your thoughts away from say, your experience of food, since Adam was told to be a herbivore. He was only to eat from plants. Meat as food which involved killing an animal was not even to enter into Adam's mind. He did not even know of this possibility. Meat from animals was not food permitted by God until after the Flood. The change then, was due to the destruction of so much plant life during the Flood. Plants alone would never again be sufficiently in abundance from then on to feed mankind. So God told Noah after he left the ark that it was now all right to eat meat. (Genesis 9:3-4).

However, there was an important condition to be met before one could eat meat. It had to be drained completely of blood, because the life of the animal is in the blood. It is recognised that the life of the animal is totally represented by its blood. So eating an animal, should involve the food gained from its flesh not its blood.

In God's eyes, it is such an offence to eat meat with the blood that, when He gave His laws to the children of Israel through his servant Moses, He said that if anyone – whether a Jew or a stranger – ate meat with the blood, they should be cut off from the people. They should be totally excluded from them (Leviticus 17:10-12). This is because the blood of the animal is its life.

So after the Flood, man was allowed to be the omnivore we now know him to be, eating plants and meats etc.

In view of God's recognition that life of a physical being is in the blood, God's action of killing the animals in order to clothe Adam and Eve with the skins was therefore a bold statement. The life blood of these animals was being shed instead of the life blood of Adam. After all God had said,

> . . . in the day that you eat of it [the forbidden tree] you shall surely die. *Genesis 2:17*

Instead, in the day that Adam ate of the tree, God killed some animals in the place of Adam. Adam did not die that day, some animals did; their life for his. Now these were animals which were part of God's creation which He had declared as good even before Adam was on the scene (Genesis 1:25).

Man, who was made in God's image, God had declared with the rest of the creation as very good (Genesis 1:31). So God made a sacrifice of animals: Animals which were part of God's good creation and had pleasing properties to Him. A sacrifice costs, and this cost God was willing to pay, in preference to the death of Adam.

This was a temporary putting off of the full requirement however; only a partial meeting of the need. A fact that can be seen in that the skins themselves were not going to last forever. The covering they provided was not going to last. Therefore the life of these animals as spilt in their blood was not going to be sufficient either.

Sure, the skins would last longer than leaves. They were a better covering but, over the years, more animals would have to be killed so as to provide new skins, not just to replace the old clothing but to clothe the sons and daughters of Adam and Eve. This was until wool, flax, cotton, etc. were discovered.

Every time blood was shed for this purpose, it could be a particular reminder of the message God had given, a testimony to it. Remember, it would not be for meat that they were to kill animals, not until the 17th Century AC (After Creation – The year of the Flood is 1656AC. This 'AC' is my own 'made up' classification).

The Message

What was this message?

This overall message greater in meaning which God was illustrating is this:

I love you so much that I will sacrifice these animals in your place – this is temporary however – but just as I have shed their blood instead of yours, so one day I will shed blood which will allow for a permanent solution; a permanent substitution. The present bloodshed is a type; it mainly provides for your physical need and is an emblem of the act of my future provision for you. Not just for the physical need but for your life itself.

This was a big event. The first killing had occurred, the first taking of life – carried out by God. Its main purpose was to spare Adam from death and it involved the shedding of life-blood in his place. God showed He was the one who would provide the means for a covering, and He was the one to provide for a life in his place.

So, did all now look rosy? Well, not quite.

Adam and Eve also had their part to play. This covering needed to be made real and effective. For the substitution to be of meaning, they now had to put on these clothes God had made: Even if this was just on the physical level.

By this act of putting on the clothes, they showed their trust in them as being sufficient for their present need. This was the part they had to play. They would have to trust, not in their own efforts (i.e. the sewing of leaves together) but in God's provision as the way forward to provide for their need, which we have seen also spoke of their need of salvation being met by God, their need of salvation from death – separation from God.

They had a practical illustration with which they could see that their own efforts would never be sufficient to meet their need of salvation.

Here we find then a first time that faith is being seen as a factor in relationships between man and God. Faith in what God was providing as sufficient for their need as evidenced by their putting on the clothes. They were by this trusting in God to supply their need, instead of trusting in their own efforts. After all, they could easily have said 'No! We will stick to our fig leaves . . .'

As we have seen, the animals being killed, their blood spilt, was a statement and a sign of God's method and purpose.

The Woman's Seed, the Final Sacrifice

As the years unfolded, God showed through His prophets more clearly about the woman's Seed and how He would suffer as the animals had suffered and be the final sacrifice (Psalm 22:1, 12-18).

One of the clearest examples of this can be seen in Isaiah:

> All we like sheep have gone astray; we have turned, every one, to his own way; and the LORD has laid on Him the iniquity of us all. *Isaiah 53:6*

The whole of Isaiah 53 shows clearly the full substitution sacrifice which was fulfilled by Jesus at Calvary (the place of crucifixion). And this was in a prophecy written about 740 years before the actual event it talks about! God could picture this event so vividly he shared many of the details to his servants, the prophets, over the centuries preceding it. These messages from God are a clear testimony to Jesus as the One to provide the final answer. We read on in Isaiah:

> . . . He was led as a lamb to the slaughter . . .
> *Isaiah 53:7*

This is echoed by John the Baptist when, on his first recorded sighting of Jesus (in John's gospel) said,

> . . . Behold! The Lamb of God who takes away the sin of the world! *John 1:29*

John, the disciple of Jesus also wrote:

> . . . He Himself is the propitiation [the substitute sacrifice] for our sins, and not for ours only but also for the whole world. *1 John 2:2*

It is no wonder then that Jesus is known in heaven as The Lamb (see Revelation 5). This provision, God had planned for from the foundation of the world. He was and is,

> . . . the Lamb slain from the foundation of the world. *Revelation 13:8*

God had allowed and planned for this from the world's inception, from its very beginning. The final sacrifice was to be His most costly. This is the genuine extent of His love towards us. This was by the giving of his life, by the actual shedding of it in his own blood, out of his many wounds on the cross.

God taught the people of Israel the value of animal sacrifices at the same time as telling them not to eat of the blood. He said,

> For the life of the flesh *is* in the blood, and I have given it to you upon the altar to make atonement for your souls; for it *is* the blood *that* makes atonement for the soul. *Leviticus 17:11*

In Hebrews we read clearly that Jesus offered up Himself as a final sacrifice for sins and that animal sacrifices had only really been pointers to His own sacrifice to come. See Hebrews 7:27, 9:22 & 26; 10:5, etc.

> For *it is* not possible that the blood of bulls and goats could take away sins. *Hebrews 10:4*

> But this Man, after He had offered one sacrifice for sins forever, sat down at the right hand of God . . .
> *Hebrews 10:12*

> . . . through the offering of the body of Jesus Christ once *for all.* *Hebrews 10:10*

See also Revelation 1:5

John 14:6 The Meaning

I think we are now ready to appreciate a different meaning of John 14:6,

> . . . No one comes to the Father except through me.

Therefore, the meaning: All who come to the Father can only do so through Jesus, because of Him as the perfect and final sacrifice for sins.

Sins which we have all committed; No man is free from having committed sin.

> . . . all have sinned and fall short of the glory of God, being justified freely by His grace through the redemption that is in Christ Jesus . . .
> *Romans 3:23-24*

So, to me, '. . . No one comes to the Father except through me' means that, if it is not for the death of Jesus for all our sins, no man could come to the Father. No one can come to the Father except for the sacrifice of Jesus in his place. For no man has the gift of eternal life granted to him except for the righteousness of Jesus being exchanged for his sin.

> For He made Him who knew no sin *to be* sin for us, that we might become the righteousness of God in Him. *2 Corinthians 5:21*

Let us then re-examine the first interpretation of a Christian as based on John 14:6,

Unless you come to know the Lord Jesus Christ (consciously) as your saviour whilst you are alive, you will not be saved.

As Paul wrote to the Thessalonians,

> Test all things; hold fast what is good.
> *1 Thessalonians 5:21*

So, let us hold fast to the good in this interpretation and discard what is not.

If someone has a living relationship with the Lord Jesus (an ongoing relationship with Him as his Lord and Saviour), then the Bible teaches that they will be saved, have everlasting life.

> For God so loved the world that He gave His only begotten Son, that whoever believes in Him should not perish but have everlasting life. *John 3:16*

Given just a very quick glance, this verse does not immediately give the idea of a living relationship.

The New Testament was originally written in Greek (Koïne Greek), and the verb 'to believe' in the above verse is in a grammatical tense, like 'future tense' or 'past tense', which is not well known or normally used in English. This tense is the 'present continuous' (that is one name for that tense) which makes the above readable as,

> . . . whoever is believing in him . . .

That is, 'whoever believes (in a continuous sense) in him . . .' or, '. . . whoever goes on believing in him . . .'

So that, having a living (an actual continuing) relationship with the Lord Jesus Christ as one's Saviour gives a present assurance of eternal life – Salvation.

This is the good to be found in the original interpretation of a Christian in the introduction. See also Acts 4:12 for the clear truth that the conscious belief in Jesus by name is the sole one given for assurance of salvation:

> Nor is there salvation in any other, for there is no other name under heaven given among men by which we can be saved. *Acts 4: 12 JM*

To those familiar with this passage it may be noticed I have made one change. I have replaced the word 'must' with 'can' to say '**can be saved**'. The Greek is *dei* which is variously translated as 'must', 'ought', 'incumbent to' but differs clearly from *anagké* which is 'must', 'obligatory' as in Romans 13:5. The emphasis is Jesus' name is the only one that can be known consciously for salvation; not that it has to be known.

The rest of the interpretation of John 14:6 to be discarded, as we have begun to see, is that someone must know the Lord Jesus Christ as their Saviour (consciously minded by name) whilst they are alive in order to be saved, i.e. the thought that everyone everywhere must do so or perish is to be discarded.

That is to say I have begun to show that a person can be saved, have eternal life, without knowing the Lord Jesus Christ as their Saviour during their lifetime.

Remember, we are mainly talking about people who have not heard about Jesus. And on top of that, we are talking about those who are not The Wicked. I discuss these in Chapter Nine. It is also worth noting here that I have presently used John 3:16 in the sense it is generally used: That is to say, the common use of 'whoever believes in Him' meaning, a conscious belief in Jesus by name. We shall see later that the context throws another light on it.

Is that it? Well, not quite, for all this has raised important questions,

* How can someone be saved without the knowledge of the Lord Jesus Christ?
* Who does God declare worthy for salvation 'in this manner'? Indeed, to whom can this be appropriated?

* Does the Bible clearly demonstrate the possibility of all this?
* What is the criterion?

5

OUTWORKING

We have already seen how Adam and Eve exercised a type of faith in order to benefit from the death of the animals killed in their place: they put on the clothes God made for them from the skins of animals. We saw that as far as their salvation was concerned, the sparing of their lives, their putting the clothes on illustrated a faith in God's action rather than theirs.

Irrespective of this wearing of the clothes however, animal lives had already been taken in exchange for theirs; blood had already been spilt. God could look at this blood and know that a substitution had already occurred. So it did not matter if they wore or did not wear what God had provided in order for their lives to be spared. It mattered as far as their clothing was concerned. They could not benefit from the skins if they did not wear them.

But it did not matter as far as shedding the animals' blood was concerned. Wearing clothes or not could not undo that. Just like you cannot un-see what you have just seen. It was as far as this was concerned an illustration.

God's View

So what was to be, and what is, God's witness to the fact that faith is active? How could God see faith in His supply for the need of salvation? How can God know that someone truly desires to go His way and, in the midst of all this, what prevented Adam and Eve from sinning again?

Indeed, they could sin again. Nothing stopped them from doing so. But, doing so would be a snub at God's goodness in letting them live and at the sacrifice He had made. It would be saying that I do not care about your provision, i.e. I want to do this thing that hurts you anyway.

It would, in effect, be asking for another sacrifice to atone for the 'second' sin, to 'pay' for it. For as the Bible also declares,

> For the wages of sin *is* death . . . *Romans 6:23*

So to demonstrate their independence, their unbelief, and their lack of love for God, all they had to do was to sin again. Simply put, lack of trust in God and His provision can be clearly shown by deliberate (with a full knowledge) acts of evil, by knowingly doing what is wrong.

Now we can begin to see the pattern of God's view: What is His witness, the visible token for God to see?

Those who live a life of deliberate sin, wilfully, show themselves to be faithless. Their actions, their words, are as a direct outcome of the state of their hearts. If deliberate sin is done, then the person concerned is without faith. And being without faith is clearly therefore the producer of offence to God. It is a continuous snub of Him and His love. For,

> . . . without faith *it is* impossible to please *Him* . . .
>
> *Hebrews 11:6*

But instead, those who seek after what is right (righteousness) and live by this show themselves to be full of faith.

This can clearly be illustrated by the first two sons of Adam and Eve, Cain and Abel.

Cain and Abel

Genesis 4 shows these two brothers as having different occupations. Cain was a tiller of the ground and Abel was a keeper of sheep. This already tells us that the value of wool for the purpose of clothing and fabricating material was now established. As time went by, they both made an offering to God.

Cain offered produce from the ground to the Lord whilst Abel offered firstlings from his flock. The Lord respected Abel and his offering, but not Cain and his.

At this juncture, it could initially be thought that God was being unfair. Cain had worked hard to make the ground produce for him. He had no modern tools to use. On the other hand, Abel did not have to work so hard, he was looking after sheep. After all, it is the sheep that do the eating and the growing of the wool . . .

At first glance, out of context, it may appear to be hard on Cain that God did not respect what he had done. But if we take a closer look at what God did and did not respect, we begin to see some of what is really going on here. What is actually written is,

> . . . the LORD respected Abel and his offering, but He did not respect Cain and his offering . . .
>
> *Genesis 4:4-5*

So irrespective of either offering, God respected Abel and not Cain. Nevertheless, considering the offerings first, we see that Abel carried out the killing, the shedding of blood of animals.

This is highly likely to have been known by both Cain and Abel as of significance to God. After all they were both old enough to work. A working age implies their having a mind able to understand various concepts including work and what it entails. A mind able also to appreciate the concepts of what they were doing in giving an offering to God. In the process of growing up, they would have been told by their parents the story of how the world came into being and about the 'first clothes' (since now wool had begun to be used). They would have said how this had involved the killing of animals in their place.

They would recall the fact that their efforts in wearing fig leaves had proved ineffective. So they could understand the concept that God's provision through shedding of an animal's blood was acceptable, but one's own effort not so. After all, in Cain offering his own produce, he had somewhat to be proud of, his own efforts in producing it. He could have something to boast about.

Abel had nothing to boast of, he was just thankful to God for the life of the lambs (or, firstlings).

We can also see that the killing of an animal in sacrifice was actually known of, as a better sacrifice, because the next mention of such an event involves Noah. When Noah left the Ark, he built an altar and sacrificed of every clean animal that had been with him (Genesis 8:20-21). If Noah had recognised the significance of offerings 16 centuries later, it is not unreasonable to recognise that both Cain and Abel had more than just an inkling of the importance of such to God. So that we have a record that,

> By faith Abel offered to God a more excellent sacrifice than Cain, through which he obtained witness that he was righteous, God testifying of his gifts; and through it he being dead still speaks. *Hebrews 11:4*

Abel's offering was therefore acceptable to God.

Let us now look closer at why God respected Abel and not Cain. Of Cain it is also written:

> . . . Cain *who* was of the wicked one [the devil] and murdered his brother. And why did he murder him? Because his works were evil and his brother's righteous. *1 John 3:12*

Here we see that before Cain murdered his brother, his works were evil. So God is seen to have respect for Abel because of his righteous works and not so with Cain because his were evil. This was also related to his sacrifice, so God was not pleased with either.

> The sacrifice of the wicked *is* an abomination to the LORD, but the prayer of the upright *is* His delight. The way of the wicked *is* an abomination to the LORD, but He loves him who follows righteousness.
>
> *Proverbs 15:8-9*

So, even though they had 'a knowledge' of the kind of sacrifice God would be more pleased about, that is the concept they knew of, that the shedding of blood was an emblem; despite this, even if Cain had done the right type of sacrifice it still would have been worthless. Even if Cain had done that right, God would not have been pleased. This is because it would be unreal for Cain; just for show. We can see this because God's sentiment is this.

> . . . I desire mercy and not sacrifice, and the knowledge of God more than burnt offerings. *Hosea 6:6*

Also see Matthew 9:13 and 12:7

This is God's feeling about sacrifices offered by the wicked:

> He who kills a bull *is as if* he slays a man; he who sacrifices a lamb, *as if* he breaks a dog's neck; he

> who offers a grain offering, *as if he offers* swine's blood; he who burns incense, *as if* he blesses an idol. Just as they have chosen their own ways, and their soul delights in their abominations, so will I choose their delusions, and bring their fears on them; because, when I called, no one answered, when I spoke they did not hear; but they did evil before My eyes, and chose *that* in which I do not delight. *Isaiah 66:3-4*

This is why, when Cain was upset about God's 'negative respect', God said to him,

> . . . Why are you angry? And why has your countenance fallen [his composure]? If you do well, will you not be accepted? And if you do not do well, sin lies at the door. And its desire *is* for you, but you should rule over it [or, Hebrew, subject unto you its desire, and you . . .]. *Genesis 4:6-7*

Clearly, this is talking about Cain himself and not just his offering. God is saying that all you have to do to be acceptable, is to change your works, from evil to righteous works: If, he also 'does well'.

But why?

Do well?

What have works got to do with being acceptable to God?

Is that not advocating a salvation by works, being accepted by God if one does well? What is right? Does not the scripture also say (Paul, writing to Christians):

> . . . by grace you have been saved through faith, and that not of yourselves [the salvation – it is by grace]; *it is* the gift of God, not of works, lest anyone should boast. *Ephesians 2:8-9*

Yes it does, the works are not therefore the primary cause of acceptance by God, but faith is. The righteous works however are the evidence, the fruit of the faith, for it is impossible to produce them without the faith.

In order for Cain to do well, there would need to be a change of heart. He would have to decide for it, i.e.

Yes. I will do right! I will stop my bad deeds and do what is right!

This involves an active choice for what is good, a decision to believe. Faith is a choice. He would need to choose to believe to do right as opposed to choose to do evil like those in the Isaiah 66:3-4 passage above.

Faith is the primary factor. It is the acknowledgment that God is right; it is choosing for Him. The works, the doing well, are fruit, the witness of the faith within. You are not saved by the doing well or not, but by the faith. They are the fruit, not the tree.

> Either make the tree good and its fruit good, or else make the tree bad and its fruit bad; for a tree is known by *its* fruit. *Matthew 12:33*

> . . . For out of the abundance of the heart the mouth speaks. A good man out of the good treasure of his

> heart brings forth good things, and an evil man out of the evil treasure brings forth evil things.
>
> *Matthew 12:34-35*

It is the faith that God recognises as the prime requisite for salvation; the good treasure of the heart. Because of faith in these being right, a good man brings forth good things. It is this heart of faith that God accepts.

> . . . the just shall live by his faith. *Habakkuk 2:4*

Because the opposite is that,

> . . . those things which proceed out of the mouth come from the heart, and they defile a man. For out of the heart proceed evil thoughts, murders, adulteries, fornications, thefts, false witness, blasphemies. These are *the things* which defile a man . . .
>
> *Matthew 15:18-20*

To conclude with Cain, it is significant that although he was the first murderer, God did not kill him, but gave him room (time enough) to turn from his evil ways and do what was right.

He gave him much opportunity to repent and thereby become acceptable. God is so loving of the sinner (He hates the sin) that He gives time to allow for a change of heart that he may be acceptable later. God hopes for the realisation to awaken that sin brings only unhappiness, as happened in the story of the prodigal (the wasteful) son (Luke 15:11-32).

God is very gracious and loving in waiting, but He is also grieved at the wrongs.

6

FAITH AND WORKS

What else does the Bible say about this faith and works?

In James we read,

> . . . faith without works is dead . . . *James 2:20*

And,

> For as the body without the spirit is dead, so faith without works is dead also. *James 2:26*

James is telling us the converse of what would be naturally thought. You would naturally think that the body is equivalent to the works and the faith to the spirit. But he says it the other way around.

The body = faith, without the spirit = works.

He is saying, without the spirit which equals the works, the body which equals the faith does not exist, is not a reality. Therefore works are evidence of faith.

It is the evidence that the body is alive.

When works are carried out naturally, as it were, they show clearly a faith within. That is to say, when works are carried out just for their own sakes, then faith is what they (the works) show the evidence of: When they are a natural outworking of the heart of faith within (that these are right).

So the natural practise of righteousness, because this is what is desired in a heart of faith, reveals a child of God. This is why John could write with confidence in his first letter,

> . . . everyone who practises righteousness is born of Him. *1 John 2:29*

Everyone, not just Christians so called, but everyone who practises righteousness, is born of Him. These are the works which reveal the identity of the faith within. This is not talking of works of the law (i.e. the Law given to Moses) or just good works (done for their own sakes) such as charitable giving/deeds. This is instead talking of practising righteousness.

The kind of works seen in Abraham who, before the Law was given to Moses, was already acclaimed by God as keeping His charge, His commandments, His statutes and His laws (Genesis 26:5):

> . . . Abraham obeyed My voice and kept My charge, My commandments, My statutes, and My laws.
> *Genesis 26:5*

Anyone who without the law (as given to Moses) practises what is within the law is acknowledged as having a saving faith, since these living practises are evidence of such.

> . . . for not the hearers of the law [of Moses] *are* just in the sight of God, but the doers of the law will be justified; for when Gentiles [non-Jews], who do not have the law, by nature do the things *contained* in the law, these, although not having the law, are a law to themselves, who show the work of the law written in their hearts, their conscience also bearing witness . . . *Romans 2: 13-15*

This is why Jesus, when talking about Judgment Day, could say to people who had not known him during their life on earth (since they did not recognise him); 'Well done – because of your righteous deeds you did to me' (Matthew 25:31-46).

We also have seen that,

> . . . the just shall live by his faith.
> *Habakkuk 2:4 and Romans 1:17 etc.*

But this faith does not exist in reality if it is fruitless. The works of righteousness done 'naturally' are evidence of this faith that God desires.

This is why Jesus also said,

> . . . I am He who searches the minds and hearts. And I will give to each one of you according to your works. *Revelation 2:23*

Speaking to Christians here, but in Psalm 7 we read,

> . . . the righteous God tests the hearts and minds.
>
> *Psalm 7:9*

Everybody's, showing God's clear view, that all hearts are seen as to what kind they are, by the kind of fruit/works which are produced in their life. God tests to make sure these are the works desired and to see the motives behind them.

Seeing that works/doings/fruits are evidence of the heart of faith within, we can also see why then we find many scriptures which talk of the final judgment as applicable according to works/doings/fruits.

Statements such as that of Jesus:

> Do not marvel at this; for the hour is coming in which all who are in the graves will hear His voice [the Son of Man's – Jesus] and come forth – those who have done good, to the resurrection of life, and those who have done evil, to the resurrection of condemnation. *John 5:28-29*

This occasion of judgment is also mentioned by Paul in his epistle (his letter) to the Romans and John in the final chapters of Revelation.

Paul, writing to the saints at Rome, said that God in his righteous judgment '***will render to each one according to his deeds***' (Romans 2:5-6). He goes on to say more specifically how this will be done. Eternal life will be given to '**those who** [my re- arrangement]

> said, 'I *go*, sir,' but he did not go. Which of the two did the will of *his* father? They said to Him [the chief priests and elders of the people – V.23], 'The first.' *Matthew 21:28-31*

The picture becomes clearer therefore that the fruit of a man's life, his works whether righteous or evil, good or bad, are statements of the heart within. It is not good enough to have a certain knowledge and experience of the Lord Jesus Christ; not if the works out of one's life are evil. This is why Jesus also said,

> Not everyone who says to Me, 'Lord, Lord,' shall enter the kingdom of heaven, but he who does the will of My Father in heaven. Many will say to Me in that day, 'Lord, Lord, have we not prophesied in Your name, cast out demons in Your name, and done many wonders in Your name?' And then I will declare to them, 'I never knew you; depart from Me, you who practise lawlessness!' *Matthew 7:21-23*

Notice that the Lord did not deny the reality of the prophecies, casting out of demons and wonders done.

The judgment however was dependent on their living practises / works / deeds / fruit (the choice is yours!). Conversely, implying clearly here, what is explained above, that all who do not know Jesus but practise righteousness will be accounted worthy of eternal life due to the faith within. See John 5:28-29 and Habakkuk 2:4.

It is worth noting here that Jesus said often not to be deceived.

> Beware of false prophets, who come to you in sheep's clothing, but inwardly they are ravenous wolves. You will know them by their fruits. Do men gather grapes from thornbushes or figs from thistles? Even so, every good tree bears good fruit, but a bad tree bears bad fruit. A good tree cannot bear bad fruit, nor *can* a bad tree bear good fruit. Every tree that does not bear good fruit is cut down and thrown into the fire. Therefore by their fruits you will know them.
>
> *Matthew 7:15-20*

This is at the heart of detecting deception.

Further Evidence

A good heart does good works, this we have seen. It produces righteous fruit by the faith that these are right. This faith is accounted to the holder for righteousness, not his own righteousness but, as we have seen, the righteousness of Jesus who has already borne the sins of the whole world.

Let us look at further scriptures. Indeed, if the above understandings are correct, it should not be hard to find in the Bible, statements about all peoples who have such a positive heart, a heart out of which positive works come, attitudes of heart compatible with God's. Compatible – or on a par with – the fruit of the Spirit. That is to say, in accord with love, joy, peace, longsuffering, kindness, goodness, faithfulness, gentleness and self-control (Galatians 5:22-23).

Well are there statements of this kind applicable to all in the Bible, applicable to Christians and non-Christians, Jews and non-Jews?

Yes, I believe there are.

In Matthew 5 we read the beginning of the 'Sermon on the mount', the portion known as the Beatitudes. I would like to touch upon a few of these.

> Blessed *are* the poor in spirit, for theirs is the kingdom of heaven. Matthew 5:3

> Blessed *are* the meek, for they shall inherit the earth.
> *Matthew 5:5*

> Blessed *are* the merciful, for they shall obtain mercy.
> *Matthew 5:7*

In verse 1, we read how there were multitudes of people. Then, we read of Jesus' disciples gathering around him. So we see Jesus teaching his disciples first and foremost. But, also he is being inclusive of all the crowds as hearers of this whole sermon.

This is unlike certain teachings he gave about his crucifixion, resurrection, the Holy Spirit and other topics at specific times, where he exclusively spoke to his disciples or just a few of them.

This sermon was for everyone to hear and, at the end of it, we read in chapter 7:28-29 that the people were astonished at his teaching because he taught with authority unlike the scribes, thus clearly confirming the fact of the whole sermon being for all to hear.

Please note, however, that even if this had only been spoken to Jesus' close disciples, it need not warrant its application being only to such as them. A teacher can speak to just a few disciples of things pertaining to all peoples, For example, in Matthew 15:15-20, Jesus explains to Peter and some disciples, truths applicable to all about 'sins which defile'.

It is bad hermeneutics – Study of the Bible within 'all' contexts – to say otherwise.

So, looking at specific beatitudes above, we see clear-cut statements which are applicable universally.

They are relevant to all.

This is very important because if it was just his disciples he was teaching, it could be a limited application. You could then be forgiven for saying, for example, that those who are poor in spirit or meek . . . are believers in Jesus and theirs is the kingdom of heaven or, they shall inherit the earth . . . But, in full context, this is not so. We can also read in Psalm 37,

> . . . the meek shall inherit the earth . . . *Psalm 37:11*

This was written before Jesus was known. Therefore, this also shows that it is not just the followers of Jesus. We can also read,

> The righteous will never be removed, but the wicked will not inhabit the earth.
>
> *Proverbs 10:30 (and Psalm 37:21-23)*

Then, to whom is it applicable?

It is plain, straightforward and clear. The poor in spirit are all who are poor in spirit: for theirs is the kingdom of heaven . . . It is for everyone. For the scripture also says,

> . . . *God resists the proud, but gives grace to the humble.* *1 Peter 5:5 and James 4:6*

Whilst this here is written to Christians, it is also written in the Psalms,

> Though the LORD *is* on high, yet He regards the lowly; but the proud He knows from afar.
>
> *Psalm 138:6*

And in Proverbs,

> . . . He scorns the scornful, but gives grace to the humble. *Proverbs 3:34*

This shows God's attitude and behaviour towards Christians and non-Christians, to everyone. It is God's reaction to all in direct accordance with the attitude of heart, whether it is either proud (arrogant, scornful, etc.) or humble (meek, lowly, poor in spirit etc.). This is why God is known as no respecter of persons.

> . . . In truth I perceive that God shows no partiality.
> *Acts 10:34*

> For there is no partiality with God. *Romans 2:11*

And equally written in Deuteronomy 10:17, 2 Chronicles 19:7, Job 34:19, Galatians 2:6, Ephesians 6:9, Colossians 3:25 and 1 Peter 1:17.

GOD TELLS US THIS TRUTH VERY OFTEN, HE REALLY WANTS US TO BELIEVE IT.

It is worth noting here that long-term consequences of these distinctly different attitudes are dependent on the person consciously holding on to them through thick and thin because it will be tested.

What else can we read of God's attitude to those who are poor in spirit, no matter who has the attitude? In Psalm 51 we find,

> The sacrifices of God [offerings to God – what really matters to Him] *are* a broken spirit, a broken and a contrite heart [/attitude] – These, O God, You will not despise. *Psalm 51:17*

In Proverbs we see,

> A man's pride will bring him low, but the humble in spirit will retain honour. *Proverbs 29:23*

In another Psalm we read,

7

A SUMMARY PLUS . . .

Bearing in mind that all written so far deals mainly with those who have not known the gospel of the kingdom, and principally, that we have been looking at 'The Righteous' among them, let us recapitulate.

The Lord Jesus Christ is the Lamb of God who took away the sins of the whole world (John 1:29, 1 John 2:2).

No one can come to the Father but by Him (John 14:6). He is the Way, for He paid the price with His own blood (Revelation 1:5). This paid in full the price of Salvation for everyone. Everyone can now have eternal life.

This is only appropriated (given) however, to those who have faith in Him, to those who truly show they desire it. It is a free gift – by sheer grace – by the love of God (Romans 3:24, Ephesians 2:8). Because,

> . . . love covers all sins.
>
> *Proverbs 10:12 also 1 Peter 4:8*

The sole requirement/quality desired in us is to have faith (Hebrews 10:38). For without faith it is impossible to please Him, but with faith it is (Hebrews 11:6, Habakkuk 2:4).

This faith is evidenced always by the fruit of one's life (James 2:18, 20). A good tree produces good fruit. A bad tree produces bad fruit. Out of the abundance of the heart the mouth speaks – and what comes out of a man defiles (or blesses) a man (Luke 6:43-45, Matthew 15:18-20).

It is never the works which are the requirement. It is always the faith within.

So since Jesus is the light that gives light to every man who comes into the world (John 1:9), whenever the choice is made to live in the light and stay there then, the evidence/the fruit will be a life of righteousness/works of such. For the opposite – the condemnation is,

> . . . this is the condemnation, that the light has come into the world, and men loved darkness rather than light, because their deeds were evil. For everyone practising evil hates the light and does not come to the light, lest his deeds should be exposed.
>
> *John 3:19-20*

So those who practise righteousness and live by this, show the faith within which God initiated – since He is the Light and they are in Him, i.e.

> . . . everyone who practises righteousness is born of Him. 1 John 2:29

> . . . he who does the truth comes to the light, that his deeds may be clearly seen, that they have been done in God. *John 3:21*

This is due to the fact that,

> . . . for in Him we live and move and have our being . . . *Acts 17:28*

So, since faith without works is dead, then the works of righteousness show the faith within, the faith desired by God as qualification for His free gift of eternal life. Even though the holder of such faith, out of which comes these works of righteousness, may not have the knowledge of God (mentally) as found in the Law and in the rest of the Scriptures (Romans 2:14): they do not know him consciously by name.

Their faith is in Christ because those who rebelled (who were without faith even before Jesus was known) were rebelling against Christ.

> . . . nor let us tempt Christ, as some of them also tempted, and were destroyed by serpents . . .
> *1 Corinthians 10:9*

This is referring to the events in the wilderness which occurred many centuries earlier as recorded in Numbers 21:5-6, long before the name of Jesus as we now know it was revealed. We find also mentioned that the prophets of Old Testament times were directed by the same Spirit of Christ who was in them.

> Of this salvation the prophets have inquired and searched diligently, who prophesied of the grace *that would come* to you, searching what, or what manner of time, the Spirit of Christ who was in them was indicating . . . *1 Peter 1:10-11*

In fact, as already indicated, we find that the Lord Jesus Christ has been and is available to all sinners to respond to, because He is,

> . . . the true Light which gives light to every man who comes into the world. *John 1:9*

Notice it says 'to every man'. Jesus, at this point in the John 1 passage, is known as the Word. He is not mentioned as becoming flesh, being born as a man, until verse 14. Also,

> Jesus Christ *is* the same yesterday, today and forever. *Hebrews 13:8*

His ministry has not changed. Even though the sinner may not recognise that it is Jesus Christ whom he is spurning when he turns his back on the light.

> For God did not send His Son into the world to condemn the world, but that the world through Him might be saved. He who believes in Him is not condemned; but he who does not believe is condemned already, because he has not believed in the name of the only begotten Son of God. And this

> is the condemnation, that the light has come into the world, and men loved darkness rather than light, because their deeds were evil. For everyone practising evil hates the light and does not come to the light, lest his deeds should be exposed. But he who does the truth comes to the light, that his deeds may be clearly seen, that they have been done in God.
>
> *John 3:17-21*

This is why Jesus said,

> . . . I am the light of the world. He who follows Me shall not walk in darkness, but have the light of life.
>
> *John 8:12*

It is interesting that coming to the light is equated with believing in the name of the only begotten Son of God. So, even though someone may not have heard about Jesus, if he follows the light, he is believing in the name of the only begotten Son of God. He is responding to the Spirit of Christ, the spirit of Jesus. This is what John also wrote in the first chapter of his gospel.

> . . . as many as received Him, to them He gave the right to become children of God, *even* to those who believe in His name: who were born, not of blood, nor of the will of the flesh, nor of the will of man, but of God. *John 1:12-13*

Remember, it is the next verse where John speaks about Jesus on earth in the flesh.

> And the Word became flesh and dwelt among us . . .
> *John 1:14*

This all explains why in John 3, Jesus gives no formula for how to be born again. There is no ritual or prayer mentioned. Indeed he says otherwise:

> The wind blows where it wishes, and you hear the sound of it, but cannot tell where it comes from and where it goes. So is everyone who is born of the Spirit. *John 3:8*

So is everyone who is born again. Being born again involves being a believer in the name of the only begotten Son of the Father which is, to come to the light. It is definitely no wonder then that John also says:

> If you know that He is righteous, you know that everyone who practises righteousness is born of Him.
> *1 John 2:29*

It is because all who practise righteousness are sowing to the Spirit, and of the Spirit will reap everlasting life.

> For he who sows to his flesh will of the flesh reap corruption, but he who sows to the Spirit will of the Spirit reap everlasting life. *Galatians 6:8*

This is why Paul could also write:

> . . . you are not in the flesh but in the Spirit, if indeed the Spirit of God dwells in you. Now if anyone does not have the Spirit of Christ, he is not His.
>
> *Romans 8:9*

So everyone who practises righteousness is born of the Spirit, born again (1 John 2:29 tying in with 1 John 5:12, et al.). See the next chapter for a fuller explanation.

God's love is so great for all of us, that He was willing and desired to make a sacrifice, a payment for us, so that we may have everlasting life, as opposed to our dying because of our sin. Remember it is a divine swap, our sin for His righteousness (2 Corinthians 5:21). Only, He will not impose it on us. It is a free gift if we truly want it. The real desire is revealed by the faith in our hearts (Habakkuk 2:4). What an immeasurable love that He should sacrifice so much for us.

The final sacrifice was to be His most costly. This is the genuine extent of His love towards us. Jesus himself declared it:

> For God so loved the world that He gave His only begotten Son, that whoever believes in Him should not perish but have everlasting life. For God did not send His Son into the world to condemn the world, but that the world through Him might be saved.
>
> *John 3:16-17*

This passage, remember, is in the context of being born again including the specifics of what the condemnation is all about. If you rebel, you turn back on the Revelation, the true light you have received, then, you enter condemnation.

Clearly demonstrating that coming to the light is the same as believing in Jesus. It is a spiritual event and not a conscious one. Not in terms of consciously knowing the name of Jesus and the gospel of the kingdom. Jesus made very plain what is the condemnation (John 3:19-20).

The Book of Life

It is no wonder then, to see God talk about this very condemnation to Moses. This was as part of a passage which makes mention of a book which God keeps. This book, this record, is known as the book of life. It is understood as a record of the names of all those who will be saved, those who will have everlasting life: Hence its name.

The occasion for this narrative between God and Moses is the first account we have where this book is mentioned. It is a passage where Moses pleads with God for His mercy on the people of Israel. They had made for themselves a statue of gold and worshipped it; turning their backs on God and what He had done for them. So Moses is here pleading on their behalf.

> . . . Oh, these people have sinned a great sin, and have made for themselves a god of gold! Yet now, if You will forgive their sin – but if not, I pray, blot me out of Your book which You have written. And the LORD said to Moses, Whoever has sinned against Me, I will blot him out of My book. *Exodus 32:31-33*

Those whom God will blot out of His book are those who have sinned against Him. This is the condemnation that Jesus mentioned: Those who deliberately turn from the light Revealed to them. This is echoed clearly in God's words through His prophet Ezekiel,

> Behold, all souls are Mine; the soul of the father as well as the soul of the son is Mine; the soul who sins shall die. *Ezekiel 18:4*

But I thought that we had all sinned. Indeed,

> . . . all have sinned and fall short of the glory of God.
> *Romans 3:23*

And,

> . . . *There is none righteous, no, not one* . . .
> *Romans 3:10*

And while we are at it, are we not all born sinners? Yes, original sin as it is known, is passed on, i.e. 'You do not teach a child to do bad, but good. The sinful nature is inbred'. (It is through the seed of the man as shown by the next verse quoted). But though these things may be true, if this is all there was to it (i.e. out of context), then no man will ever be with God in eternity. So that indeed we are told that,

> . . . just as through one man sin entered the world, and death through sin, and thus death spread to all men, because all sinned . . . *Romans 5:12*

But Paul goes on to say,

> . . . sin is not imputed when there is no law.
> *Romans 5:13*

To impute something is to take account of, to acknowledge guilt. So that sin is not remembered by God as the Old Testament puts it, when it is carried out without knowledge of transgression: Without the knowledge that you have done wrong: Against the truth that has been revealed to you. Because sin is the transgression of the law.

> . . . where there is no law *there is* no transgression.
> *Romans 4:15*

This is applicable to both the law written in Moses and the law written in one's heart as mentioned by Paul earlier, i.e. the Revelation, the light received by The Spirit of Christ (Romans 2:14-15). That is the law written in the heart.

So the sin that the Exodus and Ezekiel passage refer to was identified by Jesus as 'this is the condemnation' in John 3:19. It is a life of wickedness, because a life of evil practise is an act of specific rebellion against God, a deliberate turning away from the light revealed to the person concerned. This shows the importance and value of evangelism. It is the bringing of fresh light, of revelation and understanding, of the truths of God to the lost.

Not a Permanent Record

Now, the book of life does not have a permanent record of names. It is possible to have a name blotted out, hence Moses' plea. King David made a similar one, although it was not his own name he suggested be blotted out of the book. It was a venting of his feelings to God about a group of people who 'hated him without a cause' (Psalm 69:4).

> Add iniquity to their iniquity, and let them not come into Your righteousness. Let them be blotted out of the book of the living, and not be written with the righteous. *Psalm 69:27-28*

This actually also alludes to the truth of the statements above, that although all have sinned and all sin is offensive to God, only the purposeful sin against Him warrants blotting out of the book of life. This is why in venting his feelings David was asking God to add iniquity to their iniquity, i.e. 'Make sure they really blow it, Lord!' The last mention made of a blotting out (a rubbing out) of a name from the book of life was made by Jesus himself. He was speaking to Christians.

It makes very clear the possibility of a blotting out. There is no point in mentioning it at all, if it is not possible.

> He who overcomes shall be clothed in white garments, and I will not blot out his name from the Book of Life; but I will confess his name before My Father and before His angels. *Revelation 3:5*

A clear implication that he who does not overcome will have his name blotted out of the book of life.

Part of the wonder of God is His absolute fairness. This can be seen by the fact that when someone turns their back on wrong and turns to right He acknowledges it. He says that they will live i.e. have everlasting life due to their clear step into faith (or, return to it).

> When the righteous turns from his righteousness and commits iniquity, he shall die because of it. But when the wicked turns from his wickedness and does what is lawful and right, he shall live because of it [eternal life]. *Ezekiel 33:18-19*

I think it would then be fair to say.

The Righteous, as the Bible calls them includes Christians and some non-Christians. The Wicked includes non-Christians and some so called Christians.

Let's now see where being born again comes in.

8

THE MEANING OF BORN AGAIN

The Meaning of Born Again explains from the Bible how the experience realistically is not just about those really known as Christians, but all those who hunger and thirst for righteousness (Matthew 5:6) and as such practise it (1 John 2:29) and yet are not (yet or ever) known as Christians.

The Meaning of Born Again

The phrase 'born again' was first used by Jesus during a conversation with a Pharisee named Nicodemus. The event is recorded for us in John chapter 3.

The predominant view of this phrase is that it involves the act of becoming a Christian. It is for this reason that evangelists have often been heard to say 'Have you been born again?' Whilst this is the generally accepted view, I believe – and aim to demonstrate – that it is indeed an event which occurs to some Christians at conversion, but that it is equally experienced by many non- Christians whether they go on to become Christians or not. The reason that this has been viewed as related to the act of becoming a Christian is that verses 15, 16 and 18 mention 'belief in Him'. This is preceded in verse 14 with Jesus mentioning that 'the Son of Man must be lifted up'. Since the whole paragraph includes mention of 'born again' and belief in the Son of Man, it is easy to think that both are connected. Since the Son of Man is Jesus himself, it would be natural to understand this belief to mean the act of becoming a Christian.

However, this is a retrospective understanding, because when Jesus was talking with Nicodemus, there were no Christians per se, just Jews and Gentiles. Jesus had not yet died and risen from the dead, and the Church was not yet a reality. Furthermore, Jesus makes a clarification of what he means by 'belief in him' in verse 18, which qualifies all the previous references to this in the passage. This is what he said:

> He who believes in Him is not condemned; but he who does not believe is condemned already, because he has not believed in the name of the only begotten Son of God. *John 3:18*

This verse is then immediately reinforced by the next which starts by saying: '**And this is the condemnation . . .**' In other words Jesus immediately expands on his discourse about condemnation and the necessary belief by clarifying further what it involves. Bearing this in mind and going on to include this next verse, let us see what 'believing in the name of the only begotten Son of God' means.

In John 3:18 Jesus is saying that belief in him involves belief in '**the name . . .**' He is not saying: Believe in my title name 'Jesus', but something which was understood by the Greek speaker of the day. This phrase belief in 'the name' involves belief in the character, or attributes of the person concerned, and does not require a conscious awareness of the person himself, but the facets of their personality only, i.e. their character.

The Onoma Enigma

The Greek word for name is *onoma* and there is indeed an enigma or difficulty in understanding it. This can be seen in that it is used in several Bible passages as a reference other than to a specific name of someone or something. Indeed, there are various places where it does not refer to someone's particular autograph – but there are many where it does – hence the difficulty. Such a case in point may be seen in Matthew 18:15-20, which ends with:

> For where two or three are gathered together in My name, I am there in the midst of them.
>
> *Matthew 18:20*

Jesus' meaning here is other than to his own particular title. This can also be seen in the following passages where Jesus is praying:

> I have manifested Your name to the men whom You have given Me out of the world . . . Holy Father, keep through Your name those whom You have given Me, that they may be one as We *are*. While I was with them in the world, I kept them in Your name . . . And I have declared to them Your name, and will declare *it*, that the love with which You loved Me may be in them, and I in them. *John 17:6, 11-12, 26*

As can be seen, Jesus is not talking about the Father's title – his particular name. If he were, verse 26 would be nonsense:

> And I have declared to them Your name, and will declare . . . *John 17:26a*

In other words, if this was a particular title belonging to the Father which Jesus says he had made known, then it does not make sense that he should say he will make them know it a second time – especially when the second half of the sentence is included:

> . . . that the love with which You loved Me may be in them, and I in them. *John 17:26b*

It means in order that the Father's love and Jesus' presence may be in his disciples, this facet, or faculty, as understood by the Father's 'name' needs to be continuously made known, or appreciated. He is saying that is what enables the love of the Father and the presence of Jesus to be in the disciples.

So what does *onoma* mean in such cases? To help us, we will look at a few more such occurrences in Scripture, so that the essence of the meaning can be understood thoroughly.

> a) [Jesus is] . . . far above all principality and power and might and dominion, and every name that is named, not only in this age but also in that which is to come. *Ephesians 1:21*

Here – translated from *onomatos* – the emphasis is on an authority, a position of importance. Not unlike the English use of the word 'name' when one says 'He has made a bit of a name for himself'.

> b) [Jesus] . . . has by inheritance obtained a more excellent name than they [angels].
> *Hebrews 1:4*

Here, the meaning is more in the nature of a report; a standing; a reputation. In general, someone's particular name represents or implies a certain authority, character, rank, power, majesty, excellence. In the New Testament Greek, the use of *onoma* shows that in itself it is synonymous with these attributes. In Greek usage therefore, it can be seen that what is expressed more directly by the word 'name' itself, in English is only implied. Referring back to our example of Matthew:

> For where two or three are gathered together in My name, I am there in the midst of them.
> *Matthew 18:20*

The emphasis is on a gathering with the attitudes and frame of mind of Jesus – the attributes of Jesus' character. He said that he did not seek his own glory (John 8:50); always did those things that pleased the Father (John 8:29); he spoke the truth which he heard from God (John 8:40); etc. With these facets of attitude clearly in place, not only is Jesus in the midst of the gathering, but prayers made there will be answered, and decisions made will have heaven's full backing, for that is the context of Matthew 18:15-20.

The synonymous understanding of *onoma* in the preceding John 17 passage has to do with the character and attributes of the Father. So that when Jesus says he has revealed His name (the Father's) to his disciples, he is referring to the ways and manners of the Father – the character, traits and qualities. When he says he has kept them in the Father's name, he is saying . . . in the understanding of the grace and truth of the character of God – such that proper discerning and protection is obtained in being able to see the false and the wrong by the witness of the true and real: When he says he will make known the name, he is saying that he will make them aware of these understandings, in practise. With this meaning, we can have a better view of:

> And I have declared to them Your name, and will declare *it*, that the love with which You loved Me may be in them, and I in them. *John 17:26*

> The LORD *is* near to those who have a broken heart,
> and saves such as have a contrite spirit.
>
> *Psalm 34:18*

Isaiah tell us,

> . . . thus says the High and Lofty One who inhabits eternity, whose name *is* Holy: 'I dwell in the high and holy *place*, with him *who* has a contrite and humble spirit, to revive the spirit of the humble, and to revive the heart of the contrite ones'. *Isaiah 57:15*

And,

> Thus says the LORD: 'Heaven *is* My throne, and earth *is* My footstool. Where *is* the house that you will build Me? And where *is* the place of My rest? For all those *things* My hand has made, and all those *things* exist', says the LORD, 'But on this *one* will I look: On *him who* is poor and of a contrite spirit, and who trembles at My word'. *Isaiah 66:1-2*

Such attitude of heart will correspond with being merciful when occasion arises.

We read in one of the beatitudes that when one is merciful, God will be merciful too (Matthew 5:7). Just as when we refuse to forgive someone who has done us wrong, God cannot forgive us – applicable to Christian and non-Christian (Matthew 6:14-15).

Conversely,

> With the merciful You will show Yourself merciful; with a blameless [or, upright] man you will show Yourself blameless [or, upright]; with the pure You will show Yourself pure . . . *2 Samuel 22:26-27*

And,

> Blessed *is* he who considers the poor [or, Hebrew, the weak, or, sick]; The LORD will deliver him in time of trouble [or, Hebrew. in the day of evil]. *Psalm 41:1*

Indeed,

> Blessed *are* the pure in heart, for they shall see God. *Matthew 5:8*

This is a beatitude echoing King David's words above in Psalm 41 and in Psalm 15 where he says,

> LORD, who may abide in Your tabernacle? Who may dwell in Your holy hill? [i.e. live in God's Presence] He who walks uprightly, and works righteousness, and speaks the truth in his heart; He *who* does not backbite with his tongue, nor does evil to his neighbour, nor does he take up a reproach against his friend; In whose eyes a vile person is despised, but he honours those who fear the LORD; He *who* swears to his own hurt and does not change; He *who* does not put out his money at usury [lends with interest], nor does he take a bribe against the innocent. He who does these *things* shall never be moved. *Psalm 15*

by patient continuance in doing good seek for glory, honour and immortality' but indignation and wrath, tribulation and anguish to '**every soul of man who does evil**', '**who are self-seeking and do not obey the truth**' (Romans 2:7-9).

The above statements are further echoed by other scriptures like,

> I, the LORD, search the heart, *I* test the mind, even to give every man according to his ways, *and* according to the fruit of his doings. *Jeremiah 17:10 & 32:19*

> . . . You, O Lord . . . render to each one according to his work/deeds. *Psalm 62:12/Proverbs 24:12*

> For the Son of Man will come in the glory of His Father with His angels, and then He will reward each according to his works. *Matthew 16:27*

> For we must all appear before the judgment seat of Christ, that each one may receive the things *done* in the body, according to what he has done, whether good or bad. *2 Corinthians 5:10*

> . . . the Father, who without partiality judges according to each one's work, conduct yourselves [therefore] throughout the time of your sojourning *here* in fear.
> *1 Peter 1:17*

> And behold, I am coming quickly, and My reward *is* with Me, to give every one according to his work.
> *Revelation 22:12*

This is speaking about everyone, Christian and non-Christian. The testing mentioned is to do with enabling God to truly know the motives for what is done: Thereby ensuring him to give a truly fair judgment. That is one of the prime purposes for his searching the heart and testing the mind.

So we can see that the old saying 'Action speaks louder than words' is indeed the way God sees things. For example, if someone says they love God, but they hate their brother, then this person does not truly love God (1 John 4:20 and 2:8-10).

You can believe in God and the truth whilst not truly following God, that is, not be of God's kingdom. Just as the devils believe God, and the truth, and tremble (James 2:19). They are certainly not doers of God's will, for they rebelled and continue in that state.

But, if someone does God's will and yet does not know God, he will be accounted worthy.

Not because of his practising righteousness, but because of his heart of faith out of which it is being carried out. We can see the truth of the doing being more important than the saying illustrated by the parable Jesus gave of the father and the two sons.

> But what do you think? A man had two sons, and he came to the first and said, 'Son, go, work today in my vineyard'. He answered and said, 'I will not', but afterward he regretted it and went. Then he came to the second and said likewise. And he answered and

A full appreciation of God's heart and attitudes enables His love and Jesus' presence to be manifest.

Believing in the Name of the Son of God

With the preceding observations in mind, passages referring to a belief in 'the name of the Son of God' can be viewed in a way different from the current trend. The writer of the gospel of John also wrote a number of letters. On a par with his usage of the word *onoma* in John 17, we find this passage at the end of his first letter:

> These things I have written to you who believe in the name of the Son of God, that you may know that you have eternal life, *and that you may *continue to* believe in the name of the Son of God. *1 John 5:13*

Notice that the words 'continue to' are in italics, which signifies that these words were added by the translator. YOUNG'S literal translation of this passage (Robert Young, author of the famous concordance) reads:

---

*The Nestle-Aland Greek New Testament Text in the 26th Edition, and the United Bible Societies Greek New Testament Text in the 3rd Edition, omit the rest of this verse – This is the Greek Text from which some bible versions are translated. The Majority Text (a close consensus of the majority of Greek manuscripts) and the 'Received Text', include it, and are in line with John's use of the phrase in his gospel.

> These things I did write to you who are believing in the name of the Son of God, that ye may know that life ye have age-during, and that ye may believe in the name of the Son of God. *1 John 5:13 Young's*

Here again we see John re-emphasising the possibility of believing in more than just a 'title' by saying to those who already believe in 'the name', that his instructions in writing would help them comprehend more fully 'the name' of the Son of God. His invisible attributes and character would be better understood as a result of what he had just written. He started the letter by writing: '**God is light and in Him is no darkness at all**' (1 John 1:5). He went on to apply this by writing: '**He who says he is in the light, and hates his brother, is in darkness until now.**' (1 John 2:9). This also involves not loving the world, which is synonymous with '**. . . the lust of the flesh, the lust of the eyes, and the pride of life**' (1 John 2:15-16). He then explains how to recognise deception: '**If you know that He is righteous, you know that everyone who practises righteousness is born of Him . . . let no one deceive you. He who practises righteousness is righteous, just as He is righteous**' (1 John 2:29, 3:7).

He expanded further on this and then returned to '**. . . let us love one another, for love is of God; and everyone who loves is born of God and knows God. He who does not love does not know God, for God is love.**' (1 John 4:7-8). John finishes the letter with: '**. . . these things I have written . . . that**

you may know . . . and that you may *continue to* believe in the name of the Son of God.' (1 John 5:13). The whole letter is full of references to the character and attributes of God and how to recognise them in others. The letter also contrasts these to that of the enemy's attributes. This further attests to the 'belief in the name of the Son of God' having nothing to do with believing a 'tag-word' or 'title' of the Son of God, i.e. 'Jesus' itself, but instead his attributes and character.

John Three and the Light

In John 3 Jesus specifies clearly what one needs to believe in, to attain everlasting life. The fact that he does this by saying: '**He who believes in Him is not condemned; but he who does not believe is condemned already**,' (John 3:18) in terms of '**because he has not believed in *the name* of the only begotten Son of God.**' (italics mine) shows that an understanding from Scripture itself of 'believing in the name' is crucial – as just explained – before attempting to digest the whole passage of John 3:1-21. Let us now look at the verses in question, to see if the understanding gleaned through the preceding deliberations agrees.

As we have already stated, Jesus expands upon the condemnation referred to in John 3:18 – he says:

> And this is the condemnation, that the light has come into the world, and men loved darkness rather than light, because their deeds were evil. *John 3:19*

Jesus is saying that light of some kind has been observed but rejected in favour of darkness, by those who are then condemned by that very rejection. This is in line with not believing in 'the name', because it is an extension of the previous verse which says that a person is condemned already '**because he has not believed in *the name* of the only begotten Son of God**'. We know that this is an extension of the earlier statement, because Jesus then says: '**And this is the condemnation . . .**' (italics mine). So those who reject the light but love darkness instead, are those who do not believe, in '**the name**' – the two states are synonymous with each other. All those in this state of loving darkness show this is so in their lives '**because their deeds were evil**'. We read in verse 20:

> For everyone practising evil hates the light and does not come to the light, lest his deeds should be exposed. *John 3:20*

Everyone who loves darkness is involved in practising evil; he does not love what is right and his deeds are wicked: wholly selfish, a liar, lover of pleasure rather than others, proud of himself, etc. But, where does this light come from? In John, we read about Jesus as the Logos, the Word, and his activity is as the:

> . . . Light which gives light to every man who comes into the world. *John 1:9*

Indeed, Verse 4 tells us:

> In Him was life, and the life was the light of men.
>
> *John 1:4*

Both these verses tell us that everyone has an opportunity where the spiritual light shines in their life, contrasting with the darkness. John writes on, that as the light of the world (also known as '**the light of life**' cf. John 8:12 and Job 33:30), Jesus, the Logos, was in the world and although the world was made through him, it did not [want to] know him (John 1:10). In Verse 11 we read that he also came to his own, but his own did not receive him either. This is also mentioned by Paul, where he refers to the people of Israel, God's chosen (see Ezekiel 20:5), as rebellious: As a warning to Christians, in 1 Corinthians 10:9, Paul says: '**. . . nor let us tempt Christ, as some of them also tempted, and were destroyed by serpents**' (see Numbers 21:5-6). Paul was aware that Christ had not been received in general by 'his own' – the people of Israel.

But, there is good news, for John goes on to write (John 1:12): '**. . . as many as received Him**', – that is to say, referring to verses 10 and 11, as many in the world and of his own (the people of Israel) '**. . . He gave the right to become children of God, *even* to those who believe in His name**'. Here there is a sense in which we have come full circle, because this also identifies receiving the light as synonymous with '**believing in His name**'.

Notice in John 1, that this is before 'the Word – the Logos' is mentioned as becoming flesh (God incarnate), which is not written about until verse 14. Receiving the light, which is the same as believing in 'the name', was therefore an experience possible for anyone on earth before Jesus was born. Since Jesus is also 'the same yesterday, today and forever' (Hebrews 13:8), and the fact that by his Spirit he continues to be omnipresent – as testified by his promise 'I am with you always' (Matthew 28:20) – then this is also an experience possible for anyone on earth today. This is why I believe that it is the same experience as being 'born again'.

The receiving of him, also mentioned as 'believing in his name' is as John writes in 3:20, calling it a 'coming to the light'. It is a receiving of the Spirit of Christ by 'belief in the name'. It is therefore easy to understand that turning one's back on the light, indicates a life of evil deeds, for Paul also wrote:

> So then, those who are in the flesh cannot please God. But you are not in the flesh but in the Spirit, if indeed the Spirit of God dwells in you. Now if anyone does not have the Spirit of Christ, he is not His.
>
> *Romans 8:8-9*

Those who come to the light are those who receive the Spirit of Christ and as the last verse in the John 3:1-21 passage tells us:

> But he who does the truth comes to the light, that his deeds may be clearly seen, that they have been done in God. *John 3:21*

This corresponds to John's first letter mentioned earlier, where he writes:

> In this the children of God and the children of the devil are manifest: Whoever does not practise righteousness is not of God, nor *is* he who does not love his brother. *1 John 3:10*

Indeed, a few verses before he says that '**everyone who practises righteousness is born of Him**', (1 John 2:29) – which is where we can now really look at what Jesus said about being 'born again'. Having expanded upon the immediate context of Jesus' discussion about being 'born again' we can now see how it fits into the overall picture: The surroundings being visible, a clear view of 'born again' is possible.

Born Again – A commentary

John Three begins with Nicodemus, a teacher of religion, visiting Jesus by night. This was a good time to visit, because it was a private time away from the daytime crowds, but also because any religious leader unhappy about a visit to Jesus by a fellow teacher need not know about it. Nicodemus opens his discussion with Jesus by expressing his reason for believing that

Jesus is a man of God – hence his desire to talk with him. Jesus makes use of the occasion to express a fundamental spiritual truth:

> Most assuredly, I say to you, unless one is born again, he cannot see the kingdom of God. *John 3:3*

The Greek word for 'again' here is *anòthen.* It is also translated 'from above' in John 3:31; James 1:17; 3:15, etc. Sometimes it is 'from the first', e.g. Luke 1:3 and Acts 26:5; Also, 'from the top' in Matthew 27:51; Mark 15:38 and John 19:23. The word is translated 'anew' in Galatians 4:9, and this emphasis of a new or second time (again) is what is clearly understood in John 3:3 and 3:7, as shown by Nicodemus' immediate reply 'How . . . born . . . a second time?'.

What Jesus was effectively saying, was that you must be born a second time before you can see the kingdom of God – this was certainly how Nicodemus understood what was said:

> . . . How can a man be born when he is old? Can he enter a second time into his mother's womb and be born? *John 3:4*

So confirming the concept that this truth involved a second birthing, but expanding on the meaning of this second birth, Jesus went on to say:

> Most assuredly, I say to you, unless one is born of water and the Spirit, he cannot enter the kingdom of God. *John 3:5*

Jesus, by saying '**born of water *and* the Spirit**', (italics mine) tells us that there are two births: one is of water and one is of the Spirit. Without both, a person cannot enter the kingdom of God. The birth of water is the first birth and is the experience of everyone alive. It is the birth Nicodemus visualised with his response, i.e. born out of the waters of the womb in which he was formed. The literal Greek is 'born – that is, begotten, birthed, made up, or manufactured – out of water and spirit'. The definite article 'the' is not there preceding 'spirit'. But there is the Greek word *ek* which means 'from' or 'out of' and shows the emphasis is 'out of which one is birthed'. The birth of the Spirit (literally – out of spirit) is the second birth, and is a very different kind of birth to the first. To give more emphasis, Jesus immediately clarifies this point:

> That which is born of the flesh is flesh, and that which is born of the Spirit is spirit. *John 3:6*

In other words, the first birth – that of water – is the birth of the flesh.

By contrast, the second birth is a spiritual event, and is a prerequisite to see and enter the kingdom of God.

Jesus emphasised this when he said:

> Do not marvel that I said to you, 'You must be born again'. *John 3:7*

'Must' here is from the Greek word *dei* – 'it is needful' in the sense of 'ought'; 'it is right (and proper)'; 'correct'; 'the right (good) thing (to do)'; 'incumbent'; 'should'; 'behoveth' – as in Mark 13:14 'where it ought not'; Luke 12:12; Luke 13:14, et al. This is unlike *anagké* – 'compulsary', 'essential', 'obligatory' – as in Romans 13:5; Luke 14:18; Jude 3; Hebrews 7:12. **It is unwise therefore, to infer from John 3:7, that it is 'essential' they must be born again**: Jesus is not saying that to Nicodemus in this verse. But he already made it clear differently – i.e. it is 'essential' to be born again – *before* one can see or enter the kingdom of God, by saying you cannot unless in John 3:3 and 3:5. This is a truth from these verses, and can be stated from these; it is not from John 3:7, and cannot be said from that. It is worth noting again that in Acts 4:12: '**. . . there is no other name under heaven given among men by which we must be saved**' – must here is *dei* and not *anagké.*

So Jesus is not thereby suggesting Nicodemus is not already born again, but that it is what is needed before one can see or enter the kingdom of God.

He then goes on to say how this second birth reveals its occurrence:

> The wind blows where it wishes, and you hear the sound of it, but cannot tell where it comes from and where it goes. So is everyone who is born of the Spirit.
> *John 3:8*

Jesus is saying that although the wind exists, you can only know of its movements by the effects it creates in sound and movement, but you cannot see it come or go. This is how it is for everyone who is born of (out of) the Spirit. It is a spiritual event which you cannot understand fully – it is not a wholly conscious experience. You can only really know of its existence by its effect in and through the individual.

Being born again is not therefore something that occurs out of a conscious commitment of your will and mind to God or His Son. It is not the act of becoming a Christian.

That is a conscious act of becoming a follower of Jesus Christ, and acknowledging Him as your Saviour and Lord. The second birth on the other hand, is not a wholly conscious occurrence – the event of being born again is primarily spiritual. It occurs due to the influence of the 'surrounding' Holy Spirit, not unlike being formed in our mother's womb 'surrounded' by water, but not conscious of it.

For a person born again therefore assurance of eternal life (since it is not a wholly conscious event) is not available until they go on to know the promises of God's Word. They are understood and gained after becoming a Christian, together with all the other benefits of being a full part of the Church. This is covered in the chapter on Evangelism.

So from the passage in John 3 so far, we have seen that being born again is not the act of becoming a Christian. By Jesus' talking of belief in him in the remaining verses, the understanding arises that rebirth and belief are linked. It is due to this the idea has arisen – I believe erroneously – that being born again is equivalent to becoming a Christian. But we have seen in the preceding discussions how Jesus' own definition of what this belief in him consists of, from verse 18 onwards, is not the same as becoming a committed Christian. We saw this, because a conscious knowledge of the person believed in (i.e. Jesus) was not in question, nor any knowledge about him. The issue of belief rests wholly and only on believing the attributes of that person – the righteousness they stand for, the love, the truth, etc. This was further confirmed through John 1, because the people who lived before Jesus existed in the flesh, and could not therefore have any knowledge of him, are clearly shown as receiving him (the light). This is understood in John 1:12b as '**believe in His name**', and further confirmed in John's letter where he wrote:

> . . . everyone who practises righteousness is born of Him . . . everyone who loves is born of God and knows God. *1 John 2:29 and 4:7*

This agrees of course with the last verse of the John 3 passage in question:

> But he who does the truth comes to the light, that his deeds may be clearly seen, that they have been done in God. *John 3:21*

Done in God

Therefore, those who believe in what is right – '**does the truth**' – as the verse just quoted says, are those who receive him (the light) as John writes in 1:12. Believing in these attributes of the Son of God, releases God's enabling, and by His Spirit (out of His Spirit) the believer becomes (is begotten) a child of God. It is due to this that the deeds they do are said to be '**done in God**'. That is, the practise of righteousness (1 John 2:29) is as a result of God's working. It is therefore not surprising that Jesus said:

> Blessed *are* those who hunger and thirst for righteousness, for they shall be filled. *Matthew 5:6*

John 1 makes it clear (verses 4 & 9) that the opportunity – the reality of the possibility – of 'receiving him' is available universally. Everyone without exception is shown by these verses as availed by God of the opportunity to receive the light. It is also clearly implied in verse 12, that the 'receiving' is able to be experienced by all. What is excluded from man's ability or working, is the production by God of a 'birthing' as a child of God. This is a work of God as a direct response to the desire for righteousness. This desire is synonymous with believing 'in his name' (John 1:12b), which as we saw is also understood as 'receiving him' (John 1:12a). As a consequence of this, which is explicit in John 1:12 as the cause and effect, God enables the individual in question ('he gives the right' – Greek *exousian*, literally, 'authority') to become 'a child of God'. But this is not an authority – a right – which is left in human control; it is exercised exclusively by God. It is only God by His Spirit who does the production work, as made clear in:

> . . . who were born, not of blood, nor of the will of the flesh, nor of the will of man, but of God.
>
> *John 1:13*

The idea that we are dead and unable to receive until God's touch is erroneous and I demonstrate this in the next but one chapter entitled *Journey into Light.*

The word 'of' in this verse is from the Greek word *ek* which means literally 'out of' or 'from'. Thus this verse can be translated:

> . . . who were birthed, not out of bloods, nor out of a flesh's will, nor out of a man's will, but out of God.
>
> *John 1:13 JM*

God is the means whereby birthing of a child of God occurs. Just as commented on previously human birth occurs out of the waters of the womb – which is being born of 'bloods'. The formation of a godly spirit in man is entirely a result of being immersed in the Holy Spirit (surrounding). The only human part is the inward – the heart of heart – desire to do what is right; believing in righteousness; believing in 'the name of the Son of God'. As a result of this and this only, God then births a child of God out of that individual. This is what is meant by 'born again'.

Nicodemus' Response

Jesus having further explained the truth about the spiritual birth being like the wind's activity – you can't tell where it comes from and where it goes – 'So is everyone who is born of (out of) the Spirit'. Nicodemus exclaims:

> How can these things be? *John 3:9*

Nicodemus did not understand what Jesus was saying, and so Jesus replied:

> Are you the teacher of Israel, and do not know these things? *John 3:10*

Jesus was amazed that Nicodemus did not grasp what he was telling him. His amazement was further expressed when he continued:

> Most assuredly, I say to you, We speak what We know and testify what We have seen, and you do not receive Our witness. If I have told you earthly things and you do not believe, how will you believe if I tell you heavenly things? No one has ascended to heaven but He who came down from heaven, *that is*, the Son of Man who is in heaven. *John 3:11-13*

'Look! I am only telling you what I know and have witnessed, but you cannot take it in. If you cannot grasp the meaning of what I am telling you concerning earthly matters, how will you (go on to) understand the meanings of heavenly matters? After all, until the Son of Man, no-one has come down from heaven to talk of such' [my paraphrase]. At this point, Jesus then changes the subject and begins to talk about the Son of Man and the purposes of his coming to earth. As we saw previously, he then includes with this, the understanding of the human participation connected with his earlier reference to being 'born again'.

> And as Moses lifted up the serpent in the wilderness, even so must the Son of Man be lifted up, that whoever believes in Him should not perish but have eternal life. *John 3:14-15*

The 'present-continuous' tense of the Greek – the Greek Present corresponds more closely in meaning to the English Present Continuous than to the Present Simple – so that Young has '**whoever believes in Him**' of the NKJV quoted as '**everyone who is believing in him**' (identical for Verse 15 and Verse 16). This reveals more specifically what he is saying: 'And it is incumbent upon the Son of Man to be lifted up, just like Moses did with the snake in the wilderness, so that whoever is believing in him may not perish but have eternal life'. In other words, to ensure that those who already believe in him (as well as those who will in the future 'be believing' in him) do not perish but have eternal life, the Son of Man must be lifted up (to provide the required substitution sacrifice). At this point Jesus does not specify what this 'believing in him' entails. He only goes as far as saying that this salvation (leading to eternal life) applies to those who are already in the process of believing. He goes on to say this emphatically:

> For God so loved the world that He gave His only begotten Son, that whoever believes in Him should not perish but have everlasting life. For God did not send His Son into the world to condemn the world, but that the world through Him might be saved.
>
> *John 3:16-17*

Due to the preceding verses, the emphasis here is placed on the purpose of the work of the Son of Man. Thus this classic passage can be read:

> Because God so loved the world, in order that whoever is believing in him may not perish but have everlasting life, he gave his only begotten Son.
>
> *John 3:16 JM*

> Because of this, God did not send his Son to condemn the world but that it may be saved through him. *Paraphrase of John 3:17 JM*

Following this, Jesus then makes it clear what this specific 'belief in him' is all about. Verses 18-21, the last verses in this whole context of 'born again' have already clarified for us above what this entails on our part.

So, what was the gospel first taught by the disciples?

Jesus' Gospel

Having spent some time keeping company with and teaching his disciples, we read in Luke 9 how Jesus then sent them out to preach the kingdom of God, and to heal the sick (Luke 9:2).

> So they departed and went through the towns, preaching the gospel and healing everywhere.
>
> *Luke 9:6*

The question then arises – What was this gospel?

At this time it is evident that the disciples did not understand that Jesus would die for the sins of the world, and that he would then rise again. Indeed, Jesus later mentioned these things to come, but they could not take it in: '**They understood none of these things; this saying was hidden from them, and they did not know the things which were spoken**' (Luke 18:31-34). So the gospel which the disciples were preaching earlier had nothing to do with the 'traditional gospel' as related by many Christians. Jesus' commandment to the disciples to teach the nations (Matthew 28:19) did not include this 'traditional gospel' either, but only what he had commanded them – and what was this? What did the disciples know as 'the gospel' when they were sent out?

It would have been nothing more than the teachings of the Sermon on the Mount, the parables, and the other truths that Jesus taught and demonstrated about the kingdom of God. It did not particularly involve any other doctrine or tradition. But it did encompass how to treat your fellow man and how to love – truly from the heart – and how to love and live for God. They were teachings which enlightened the mind on the ways and attributes of God – which is why Jesus had said during his Sermon on the Mount:

> Be ye therefore perfect, even as your Father which is in heaven is perfect. *Matthew 5:48 AV*

Is it any wonder then, that throughout the pages of the gospels, we find Jesus calling on his listeners to stop doing evil deeds and to be pure minded. Nothing of wickedness or unrighteousness had any part in his character. Deliberately allowing these in one's life is active unbelief '**in the name of the only begotten Son of God**' . . . loving of '**darkness rather than light because their deeds were evil**'. Conversely, a desire for what is right is real faith '**in the name of the only begotten Son of God**' and shows them as someone who '**does the truth**'; someone who comes '**to the light**' and is not afraid, that '**his deeds may be clearly seen**' for '**they have been done in God**' (John 3:18-21). That is a person who is born again:

> If you know that He is righteous, you know that everyone who practises righteousness is born of Him.
> *1 John 2:29*

9

THE WICKED

Under discussion so far has been the premise, the basis by which non-Christians may 'get to heaven' as found in the Bible.

Some may then say: So who is not saved? Does this mean all will eventually get to heaven? That is to say, is this a form of universalism?

Universalism is the name given to the belief that all men will eventually be saved. One categorical statement made so far has been that:

Having a living (an actual continuing) relationship with the Lord Jesus Christ as one's saviour gives assurance of eternal life (of salvation).

I have discussed how this does not exclude from salvation some who have no such relationship or knowledge consciously of the Lord Jesus Christ. Another categorical statement I would now like to make is:

All who live a life of wickedness (sin) are destined for everlasting damnation – the final hell.

This is also known as the lake of fire. I say this to clearly show that universalism is not my belief, but instead my aim is in the balancing of the Word of truth – The Bible.

The crux, the core of this statement as to whom this applies depends on the meaning of 'a life of wickedness'. This I have shown by specifying it as an act of specific rebellion against God, a deliberate turning away from the light Revealed to the person concerned.

Paul wrote that God,

> . . . desires all men to be saved . . . *1 Timothy 2:4*

Indeed God spoke through the prophets of old,

> . . . '*As* I live', says the Lord GOD, 'I have no pleasure in the death of the wicked . . .' *Ezekiel 33:11*

God is not pleased when the wicked die. He has no pleasure in it. They have exhausted all the time God had given them where they could have turned to the light. His heart is breaking to see that they have remained in this state. Therefore now the big question is this: If God loves all, if He desires all to have eternal life, if Jesus' blood shed is sufficient to cover all sins of everyone, then why will there be some in hell? Why is it, when God himself does not desire it?

There is only one reason.

This reason is that it is only because they have chosen to do so, that is the answer. It is the wicked who have chosen to exclude God from their lives by turning their back on the light. That is the clear choice they have made.

> . . . [They] are those who rebel against the light;
> they do not know its ways nor abide in its paths.
>
> *Job 24:13*

God in His whole nature is inclusive, not exclusive. It is the wicked who exclude themselves. It is not God's desire, it is theirs. He releases them to what they clearly show they desire.

God does not impose His will on anyone. He will not force into heaven (His kingdom) anyone who does not want to be there. The fruit of the Spirit which includes gentleness and self-control are a clear indication of this (Galatians 5:22-23). God exercises self-control in the clear knowledge that this is what the wicked want. He knows this from having put stumbling blocks in their paths of wickedness, by having tested them on their path, the path away from His light.

But isn't there such a thing as God's irresistible grace?

No, because the Bible teaches that there is an attractive grace, drawing men to it, but that it can be resisted.

> . . . the goodness of God leads you to repentance . . .
>
> *Romans 2:4*

It is attractive, but God and it can be resisted. That is why we are instructed:

> Do not quench the Spirit. *1 Thessalonians 5:19*

So much so, that as already stated in Chapter One, Christians themselves can close the door to Jesus.

> Behold, I stand at the door and knock. If anyone hears My voice and opens the door, I will come in to him and dine with him, and he with Me.
>
> *Revelation 3:20*

God requires us all to have faith.

> But without faith *it is* impossible to please *Him* . . .
>
> *Hebrews 11:6*

Faith is a choice, just like heresy is a choice. You can only choose what is put before you to choose. By his Spirit he reveals himself, by pointing to His creation and by the other good news he puts before us (see Chapter Eleven for further details).

So that, where there is condemnation it is the active choice of those who receive it. They choose to turn away from the light revealed to them, from the revelation they have received. It is as God put it, a personal sin against him. It is their choice not God's. As we saw:

> . . . this is the condemnation, that the light has come into the world, and men loved darkness rather than light, because their deeds were evil. For everyone

> practising evil hates the light and does not come to the light, lest his deeds should be exposed.
>
> *John 3:19-20*

What light? Jesus, who is by his Spirit,

> . . . the true Light which gives light to every man who comes into the world. *John 1:9*

I have explained how Jesus, has through the ages been the light, 'the name' as it is often described in John's gospel and letters (e.g. 3:18) as revealed by the whole context. He is the light that men either listened to or spurned. So we see that it is what they have chosen. It is they, the wicked, who do not want to be in the light, which is why Jesus also said:

> . . . those who have done good [will come forth], to the resurrection of life, and those who have done evil, to the resurrection of condemnation. *John 5:29*

It is no wonder then, knowing that God loves us all so much, that he puts stumbling blocks in the way of all wicked individuals so that we might realise our folly and do right. But after a few times, He releases us to our wickedness because that is what we persist in showing we want.

> Behold, God works all these *things*, twice, *in fact*, three *times* with a man, to bring back his soul from the Pit, that he may be enlightened with the light of life. *Job 33:29-30*

Comparing this quote with John 8:12 we can see – the light of life – is again talking about Jesus, the light of the world: Walking in the light has been the same through all ages. It is talking about walking in the Revelation which Jesus has been by His Spirit. This is what Jesus said:

> . . . I am the light of the world. He who follows Me shall not walk in darkness, but have the light of life.
>
> *John 8:12*

The Job passage is a statement made by Elihu, a friend of Job. The immediate context (verses 14-28) talks of God's ways of trying to turn someone from sin, allowing pain or trouble to occur in order to humble the person so that they repent (verses 16-20), change their ways.

However, once they are truly seen to want this life of sin, God releases them into it because they are showing no sign of wanting otherwise.

It still gives God no pleasure.

There are many passages that talk of God allowing trouble to enable a form of common-sense to be reached, so a return may be occur, let alone several clear mentions that God releases people to their choice of future. I do not wish in the framework of this book to go at lengths on these specifics. Instead here are a few passages for the perusal of the reader about God putting stumbling blocks in sinners' way so that they might turn from this path: Amos 4:6-11, Jeremiah 5:3, Haggai 2:17.

There are passages where God is actually speaking to his own people, Israel, to try and enable them to see their error, but a principle is established, as shown by the Job passage above, that God does this to all for a limited time. Indeed God resists the proud and He hides his face from them. And since he is the source of all that is good, this pride makes us to walk into what is not good. We are clearly told:

> Draw near to God and He will draw near to you . . .
>
> *James 4:8*

This clearly implying the reverse that turning our backs on God prevents him turning his face toward us, as explicitly confirmed by God's refusal to hear prayers of the wicked: That is to say, God will not hear what you say if your life does not tell him you want it (hence, incidentally, part of the value in fasting). Here is a list of passages to show God will not hear these kinds of prayers: Zechariah 7:13, Jeremiah 11:11, Jeremiah 14:12, Proverbs 1:28-29, Ezekiel 8:18, Isaiah 1:15, James 4:3.

I have listed passages which show God putting stumbling blocks in the pathway of people to try and help them 'come to their senses', and several for His unwillingness to respond to prayers when persistent sin occurs. Here is now a list of a few passages showing God releasing people into their clear desire and purpose to sin: Romans 1:24, Psalm 81:11-12, Acts 7:42, 2 Thessalonians 2:10-12.

Probably the best example of all the above, showing clearly God's heart in all of this, is the story Jesus gave of the Prodigal (the wasteful) son in Luke 15:11-32.

In this parable we see the father of the two sons as representing God. We see that one of his sons, one of his own children, no longer wanted to live with his father and work with him. The father did not leave, his son left. It is not God who desires this event.

The son was still his son, but once he had left (after a clear decision process to leave) this very son was reckoned as dead and lost. This is what the father said to both his servants and the other son who had stayed with him. Once the son who had originally left, returned, turning his back on the life away from the father, the father said,

> . . . this my son was dead and is alive again; he was lost and is found. *Luke 15:24 & 32*

How does God operate like this, this decision process to leave, putting stumbling blocks in the way before releasing the wicked? We have a number of scriptures above to show this. This is how it works in this story.

In the parable of the prodigal son, we see the son who desired to leave not able to do so until he had 'cleared it' with his father.

> . . . A certain man had two sons. And the younger of them said to *his* father, 'Father, give me the portion

> of goods that falls *to me.*' So he divided to them *his* livelihood. *Luke 15:11-12*

This is not to say that the father desired or wanted this to happen. He would have liked his son to stay and be with him. The father did not desire his son's departure, but went along with the son's genuine wishes.

However before the son could go, the father was involved in releasing him. By this, ensuring that was what the son truly wanted to do. This is what I mean by the son 'clearing it' with his father. It is a clarification process if you like.

Dividing the inheritance involved planning, time and effort. A working out of what needed dividing up was involved, how to do it and organising the doing of it. This, taking time and effort would also involve the emotions of those involved. Possessions and goods acquired by descent (from fore parents) or by work over the past being a part of the life and soul of the owner, full of memories of people and various occasions.

So, if (for example) the son's wish had been made in haste, then this process gives room to realise his hastiness, a type of cooling off period. If the son felt for his father's feelings, those would come to the fore (the son's feelings) in seeing his father making arrangements for hard-earned possessions to be divided up or sold, etc.

In this way it would not be a sudden release or a very quick departure. It would become clear to both parties concerned, the father and the son, that this was the full intent and purpose of the son.

The son's heart would become in full view as to its contents. The motives, purposes and desires would be known, that is, to really want to depart and only go his own way, or not.

This parable used in this way serves well to illustrate what I have been trying to explain above. The beauty of this particular story though is that the son did eventually return.

> . . . for him who is joined to all the living there is hope . . . *Ecclesiastes 9:4*

All is not lost, there is hope, whilst the wicked are alive because God's heart is still wanting them to be His sons (alive and 'found' – in God's purposes for them).

Fruit of Walking Away

What are the sins, the kinds of offence which can be seen in a life of rebellion?

There are a great many lists of these in the Bible. There is a good number of compact ones of those in the New Testament. Again I do not wish to go on at length about these, so here is a list of some passages with more detail. Matthew 15:19-20, Mark 7:21-23, Romans 1:29-32, Galatians 5:19-21, Colossians 3:5-8, 2 Timothy 3:2-4, Revelation 21:8, et al. I will quote one uttered by Jesus:

> For from within, out of the heart of men, proceed evil thoughts, adulteries, fornications, murders, thefts, covetousness, wickedness, deceit, licentiousness, an evil eye, blasphemy, pride, foolishness. All these evil things come from within and defile a man.
>
> *Mark 7:21-23*

What I would like to say is that these are relevant only if they are a living practise, if it is a natural fruit out of a faithless heart, that is to say, 'Are they fixtures and fittings or a passing trolley'.

This is why Paul talks about those who practise such things (the wrong things) will not inherit the kingdom of God. It is a practise, a regular facet or fruit of the life concerned. I see a life of wickedness as the practising of sinful deeds. This is not just talking about evil actions but would also include acts of deliberate omission.

> . . . to him who knows to do good and does not do *it*, to him it is sin. *James 4:17*

This is talking about something which is known: If you like, an actual event for which you are able and available to do, an event which in itself calls on you to act.

A good example is the story of the Good Samaritan.

> . . . A certain man went down from Jerusalem to Jericho, and fell among thieves, who stripped him of

> his clothing, wounded *him*, and departed, leaving *him* half dead . . . Now . . . a certain Samaritan, as he journeyed, came where he was. And when he saw him, he had compassion *on him*, and went to *him* and bandaged his wounds . . . and took care of him . . . *Luke 10:29-37*

The wounded man was unable to help himself. He was situated in the way of travel of the Samaritan. The Samaritan could have turned a blind eye. But clearly there on his route, was someone with a real need which he could do something about.

This is what I call a God-given opportunity to help. He was equipped to do so and it coincided with being along his actual path. That is what I mean about something which is known. He was the one there to help.

Failing deliberately to help when there is such an opportunity is a sin.

If opportunities of this kind occurred regularly and the habit, the practise, was to ignore these then they show clearly the character of the person concerned as evil, a clear characteristic of a life of wickedness.

> . . . those who practise such things will not inherit the kingdom of God. *Galatians 5:21*

This follows a list Paul makes of the works of the flesh. He says the same in Romans following another list of wrong doings.

> . . . those who practise such things are worthy of death . . . *Romans 1:32*

This is talking about sins which are an integral part of the life of the wicked person. This is how Jesus described it,

> You have heard that it was said . . . *'You shall not commit adultery'*. But I say to you that whoever looks at a woman to lust for her has already committed adultery with her in his heart. And if your right eye causes you to sin, pluck it out and cast *it* from you; for it is more profitable for you that one of your members perish, than for your whole body to be cast into hell. And if your right hand causes you to sin, cut it off and cast *it* from you; for it is more profitable for you that one of your members perish, than for your whole body to be cast into hell.
> *Matthew 5:27-30*

Jesus is not talking about your actual physical body. He equates an area of your life which causes you to sin as an integral part of your character: As a living organ connected to your life, your being. The example he gave was of lusting after a woman. Now if this is a clear problem area in someone's life, looking at women to lust after them, then it is like having a bad eye. As if the eye concerned was cancerous and this affected what you saw through it.

Jesus is saying that, if you have such an offending part of your life, your attitude to it is to be as firm and resolute in not wanting it, just as if it was a cancerous part of your physical body. Just as if your hand had gangrene and the only way to stop it spreading or affecting the whole of your body is to cut it off.

The attitude to any known sin in our lives needs to be like this so that we can be free from it. We need to be firm and resolute in choosing not to sin. At such times we also need the assistance of the expert Surgeon. He is only a prayer away.

Hell

Jesus mentioned in the above passage a place called hell. In view of this chapter involving the wicked, I think it necessary to discuss hell. In a parallel passage to the one in Matthew, Jesus tells us a bit more about this place.

> And if your eye makes you sin, pluck it out. It is better for you to enter the kingdom of God with one eye, than having two eyes, to be cast into hell fire – where '*their worm does not die and the fire is not quenched*'. *Mark 9:47-48*

Jesus is telling us that hell will have a fire that will never go out. This is why he says the fire is not quenched. He is also saying that the worm of those in this place will not die. That is to say that in the context of talking about the offenders, those who hold on to their offensive life, 'they' will be forever in this place.

They chose to hold on to this life and this is the consequence. We know that it is them who remain there because Jesus says clearly '**. . . their worm does not die . . .**' It is not anyone else's worm it is 'their' worm. If it had said 'the worm' you could be forgiven for thinking that the means of suffering, of rotting away, was there but it might not be permanent for the occupants.

The pronoun 'their' refers back to the offenders mentioned in the previous sentence. The fact that it is their worm and that it (their worm) shall not die means that they will always be 'rotting in there'.

This is solemn stuff which is probably why I do not relish talking too much about it. It is necessary however to give '**the whole counsel of God**' (Acts 20:27), and this is why I try to talk about this here.

'**Their worm does not die and the fire is not quenched**' is a direct quote by Jesus of Isaiah 66:24. It is the last verse of this book of 66 chapters. This work, by this 'major' prophet has been likened to a mini Bible. One example of this is that it has 66 chapters. The Bible after all has 66 books. Another is that in the midst of the last two chapters of Revelation and the last two of Isaiah there is a clear reference to the new earth God will create. (See the Preface).

The very last whole paragraph of Isaiah as it is found in the Hebrew, as originally written, has been divided up into the last three verses of the book in our translations. This is what it says in its original whole,

> 'For as the new heavens and the new earth which I will make shall remain before Me,' says the LORD, 'So shall your descendants and your name remain. And it shall come to pass *that* from one New Moon to another, and from one Sabbath to another, all flesh shall come to worship before Me,' says the LORD. 'And they shall go forth and look upon the corpses of the men who have transgressed against Me. For their worm does not die, and their fire is not quenched. They shall be an abhorrence to all flesh.
>
> *Isaiah 66:22-24*

Now if this is the finality of all things like the last chapters of Revelation seem to show, then this hell is going to be a place which will be visible from this new earth. The new earth being in these passages the final habitation mentioned in the Bible for God and His followers. This being so there can be little doubt that what Jesus was alluding to was a permanent existence in hell for the wicked. He not only mentions their worm, but also their fire (as per Isaiah). We know this is to be a conscious existence because this is made clear for the devil. It is also clear that wicked men will share in exactly this same fate with the devil.

> . . . the devil, who deceived them [the nations], was cast into the lake of fire and brimstone where the beast and the false prophet *are*. And they will be tormented day and night forever and ever.
>
> *Revelation 20:10*

The beast and the false prophet are recognisable as men and they will be tormented forever and ever. They are clearly shown as being in conscious torment. I appreciate having just said these two characters are men may not be clearly visualised by all. Suffice it to say that a perusal of the statements made about them in Daniel and Revelation will show that either one or both of these individuals are clearly fellow humans. At least one of them is also known as the Antichrist, or the son of perdition.

The torment '**forever and ever**' finds the word 'forever and ever' translated from the Greek *aiònos* twice. The Hebrew Old Testament has 'ever and ever' translated in 29 places to my count. This is from a number of Hebrew words in different combinations: the majority being 5769 + 5703 (Strong's lexicon numbers: James Strong's Concordance and Dictionaries Copyright 1890 Madison, N.J.). Together these two mean 'out of sight/beyond view' and 'perpetually so (onwards)' added together to mean eternity onwards.

I have checked every place where 'ever and ever' is translated from this Hebrew within the Greek of the Septuagint (LXX) – the O.T. Greek version the 1st Christians used – And, every time *aiònos X* 2 occurs.

It is thereby fully to be appreciated that whenever 'ever and ever' is found in the New Testament – since every place *aiònos* X 2 is employed, it is therefore to be fully understood as perpetually so (onwards) and nothing less. Universalists argue that *aiònos* means different things: that is true, but on its own only.

When two are used as in this verse, it is a clear unambiguous reflection of the Septuagint use translating every occurrence of the Hebrew of 'ever and ever' meaning perpetually so (onwards).

> And the devil, who deceived them, was cast into the lake of fire and brimstone where the beast and the false prophet *are*. And they will be tormented day and night forever and ever. *Revelation 20:10*

So that it can be seen that all the wicked going there will be in a conscious existence, they will be in the same condemnation as the devil (1 Timothy 3:6) for ever and ever: sober words.

So What Now?

The best person to speak into this is God himself.

> '. . . *As* I live, says the Lord GOD, 'I have no pleasure in the death of the wicked, but that the wicked turn from his way and live. Turn, turn from your evil ways! For why should you die . . . The righteousness of the righteous man shall not deliver him in the day of his transgression [a conscious deliberate turning away – the outcome of a clear decision process]; as for the wickedness of the wicked, he shall not fall because of it in the day that he turns from his wickedness; nor shall the righteous be able to live because of *his righteousness* in the day that he sins. When I say to the righteous

that he shall surely live, but he trusts in his own righteousness and commits iniquity, none of his righteous works shall be remembered; but because of the iniquity that he has committed, he shall die. Again, when I say to the wicked, "You shall surely die," if he turns from his sin and does what is lawful and right, *if* the wicked restores the pledge, gives back what he has stolen, and walks in the statutes of life without committing iniquity, he shall surely live; he shall not die. None of his sins which he has committed shall be remembered against him; he has done what is lawful and right; he shall surely live.'

Ezekiel 33:11-16

10

JOURNEY INTO LIGHT

In this chapter you will read from the bible that man is not wholly dead. A total spiritual death sometimes spoken of as 'total depravity' or 'total inability' is not biblical. What the bible shows instead is that from his natural birth onwards there is a journey into Light.

The Bible tells us,

> . . . God is light and in Him is no darkness at all.
>
> *1 John 1:5*

Since He is also known as,

> . . . the Alpha and the Omega, the Beginning and the End. *Revelation 21:6*

It then follows that any journey into Light starts and ends with God. The journey started at our creation.

> In the beginning . . . God said, 'Let Us make man in Our image, according to Our likeness . . .' So God created man in His *own* image; in the image of God

> He created him; male and female He created them . . . the LORD God formed man *of* the dust of the ground, and breathed into his nostrils the breath of life; and man became a living being. *Genesis 1:1, 26-27, 2:7*

Now this is not recorded for any other of God's creatures. So, on two counts we are different from all others. First we are created in God's image and second, He has breathed life into us. God is not on record as breathing of Himself into any other creature. And there is no other understood as being made in His image. Whatever we may think of our fellow man there is no other creature like him in this respect.

The journey then begins with a relationship with God which involves His instruction.

> Then God blessed them, and God said to them, 'Be fruitful and multiply; fill the earth and subdue it; have dominion over the fish of the sea, over the birds of the air, and over every living thing that moves on the earth.' *Genesis 1:28*

God also tells our first parents that the food available to them involves the vegetation that has been created. And that this is the same for all the animals. This was to change after the Flood, but that is how it began. He then places Adam, before Eve came along, into a garden as a first dwelling place – A home to begin life on earth and to look after. In this garden He also placed two trees – The tree of life and the tree of knowledge of good and evil. Of this second tree the Lord said:

> . . . Of every tree of the garden you may freely eat; but of the tree of the knowledge of good and evil you shall not eat, for in the day that you eat of it you shall surely die. *Genesis 2:16-17*

The Literal Hebrew, the language the Old Testament of the Bible is written in is like this:

> . . . in the day that you eat of it dying you shall die. *Genesis 2:17*

The Lord begins also to spend time with Adam and in this time He brings before Adam animals and He enjoys seeing what Adam calls them. On another occasion, as the Lord desired to spend time with Adam, we read:

> . . . they heard the sound of the LORD God walking in the garden in the cool of the day, and Adam and his wife hid themselves from the presence of the LORD God among the trees of the garden. Then the LORD God called to Adam and said to him, 'Where *are* you?' *Genesis 3:8*

Eve was with Adam now and they hid themselves because they had eaten of the forbidden fruit. This had caused them to realise they were naked and in this recognition they decided to hide. The journey away from God had begun.

Were they now dead?

No. We saw that God said a process of dying would take effect:

> . . . in the day that you eat of it dying you shall die.
>
> *Genesis 2:17*

So they did not die completely, but part of them began to die. They did not die on that day physically nor, did they die wholly spiritually. We not only know that they did not die physically and that this was because others had their blood shed in their place. But we also know that spiritually the life within was not extinguished.

In the recognition that Adam and Eve now needed clothing we read,

> . . . for Adam and his wife the LORD God made tunics of skin, and clothed them. *Genesis 3:21*

God's use of animal skins, leather, meant as discussed earlier, that He is on record as the first person to shed blood. This blood shed meant the life of those animals was shed in place of the life-blood of Adam and Eve. So we see that there was a way to spare them from death. By temporary substitution – a permanent one was to follow.

But were they now spiritually lifeless?

Were they unable to respond to God without some fresh input on His part? Certainly dimmed spiritual insight and deception had begun to take effect in their lives from the moment the Devil's lies took hold – Thus veiling their eyes to the light for their way. But God is seen as aware and expectant, of a spiritual ability within man throughout scripture: An ability that could allow for more light to be accessed.

How can this be?

We saw that in the beginning at Creation God not only made man in His own image, but He breathed life into him. This did not occur with any other being. Of all the creatures God has made we are the only ones recorded as God having breathed life into (Genesis 2:7). God implanted a piece of Himself in us. Can God die? No.

But this life in us is dependent on us to enable its growth or, our eventual separation from 'it'. Our receipt and acceptance of Him as described in John 1:12 enables God's subsequent (gift) right to become children of God.

Our rejection of Him eventually causes what we 'have' to be taken away. Jesus speaks about what we 'have' in this way:

> . . . whoever has, to him more will be given, and he will have abundance; but whoever does not have, even what he has will be taken away from him.
>
> *Matthew 13:12; Matthew 25:29; Mark 4:25; Luke 8:18; Luke 19:26*

If you have a desire for righteousness, then more will be given you. If you do not, then your ability to desire for righteousness itself will be taken from you. God will test you to see what is in your heart and what you sow out of that heart you shall reap (Galatians 6:7-8; Revelation 2:23 et al.).

Scripture is clear that everyone 'has' even though they may not yet be born again. No one is totally dead that they have nothing with which to respond to the Light who is in the world. To respond to Jesus as,

> . . . the true Light which gives light to every man who comes into the world. *John 1:9*

How Do We Know This?

One pointer as shown is Jesus saying 'whoever does not have, even what he has will be taken away from him'. Everyone 'has' something which can eventually be taken away.

Animals do not share this 'life'. They have not been 'breathed' into by God. Now in Hebrew 'breath' is synonymous with 'spirit'. And since God is a Spirit, this is what is in us all to the measure that scripture indicates. Unlike animals, when we die, this 'spirit' returns to God. Thus showing itself to have remained untainted by 'the fall' or, sin. Regarding this difference this is the record:

> All go to one place: all are from the dust, and all return to dust. Who knows the spirit of the sons of

> men, which goes upward, and the spirit of the beast, which goes down to the earth? *Ecclesiastes 3:20-21*

> Then the dust will return to the earth as it was, and the spirit will return to God who gave it.
> *Ecclesiastes 12:7*

We know this is talking about God's spirit 'part' within us because the scripture also shows this:

> If He should set His heart on it, *if* He should gather to Himself His Spirit and His breath, all flesh would perish together, and man would return to dust.
> *Job 34:14-15*

This is why God is known as Father of all, because He is:

> . . . the God of the spirits of all flesh . . .
> *Numbers 16:22*

> . . . the LORD, the God of the spirits of all flesh . . .
> *Numbers 27:16*

The idea that the disobedience of Adam caused the complete tainting of all of his being and his posterity is false. The part or aspect of man's being which is untainted is that which enables receipt and response to God's revelation to all: The area of our being which is conceived with us at the inception of our existence. This is what we all 'have' as Jesus put it when he said 'even what he "has" shall be taken away' as quoted above.

When God gave the instruction not to eat of the fruit He did not say you shall die and that this death was going to render ineffective spiritual activity or awareness without new and fresh input by God. As we saw the literal Hebrew of what God said to Adam is '**in the day that you eat of it *dying you shall die***' (Genesis 2:17 – my emphasis) as explained in many Bible margins. Adam did not die on that day, but a process of dying began. A process that did not 'touch' or affect the life God placed within which can not die. But – we – can separate ourselves from it. And this then causes what Jesus said '**even what he has will be taken away from him**'.

We know that Adam still had a means to do what was right. We know this because when God spoke to Adam's first son Cain, God told him that if he did what was right he would be accepted? And, that this would prevent sin from having its way. The express result being that Cain would be acceptable to God.

If this ability is in Cain, it is in Adam and his posterity: all of us.

> . . . the LORD said to Cain . . . If you do well, will you not be accepted? And if you do not do well, sin lies at the door. And its desire *is* for you, but you should rule over it. *Genesis 4:6-7*

There is a call of God and expectation of this ability throughout scripture even amongst the most wicked.

> . . . if a wicked man turns from all his sins which he has committed, keeps all My statutes, and does what is lawful and right, he shall surely live; he shall not die. None of the transgressions which he has committed shall be remembered against him; because of the righteousness which he has done, he shall live. 'Do I have any pleasure at all that the wicked should die?" says the Lord GOD, '*and* not that he should turn from his ways and live?'
>
> *Ezekiel 18:21-23*

Even in a passage popular as a 'proof text' to say otherwise there is clear inherent ability alluded to. I am referring to Ephesians 2:1 which in English reads '**. . . you *He made alive*, who were dead in trespasses and sins . . .**'

This is read by some as saying that God made alive dead people: Folk with no life to respond to God with. Whereas actually the 'in' here is only valid from the Greek original if understood 'whilst in'. The New Testament section of the Bible was first written in Greek. The Greek for 'in' is *en*, but it is not found in Verse One. It can be found in Verse Two. The reason it is used in the English translation is that the words '**the trespasses and the sins**' are in a grammatical form known as the Dative. The use of the Dative here is to indicate *the means by which* they were '**dead**'. This is known as the instrumental use of the Dative.

So that, it is *whilst active in* trespasses and sins that they 'were dead': Clearly implying an ability to not be active in sin. Ephesians 2:1 therefore is an indicator of ability to turn from sin.

Yes, the Bible tells us we are all sinners for '**. . . all have sinned . . .**' (Romans 3:23), but as shown above it also says we are able to turn from sin. It is also mentioned that '**. . . in Adam all die . . .**' (1 Corinthians 15:22) but, by the measure of the Spirit within each of us we can look to Christ to have Life.

What of the gospel?

There is more than one gospel mentioned in the Bible. The word stands for 'glad tidings' or 'good news'. But, it is more commonly used to represent the message of Jesus as saviour of the world by which men need to be saved. The Bible does not restrict it in this way and shows that other good messages positively responded to also lead to salvation. It is responded to by many on their journey into Light. Paul said of one good news message,

> So then faith *comes* by hearing, and hearing by the word of God. But I say, have they not heard? Yes indeed: '*Their sound has gone out to all the earth, and their words to the ends of the world*'
>
> *Romans 10:17-18*

He is alluding to one of the gospels mentioned in the Bible. I go on to discuss this in the next chapter: *A Word about Evangelism*

11

A WORD ABOUT EVANGELISM

If as already explained in the main text, it is not absolutely necessary to come to know Jesus Christ as one's saviour and Lord in order to be saved then, what is the point of evangelism?

Indeed, what is the purpose of evangelism? The quickest way to answer that is to ask the question: why did God want Cornelius, the Roman centurion, to know about His Son, since Cornelius already was accepted by Him (he was acceptable to God)?

As we saw, before Peter talked about Jesus to Cornelius and his companions he said,

> . . . In truth I perceive that God shows no partiality. But in every nation whoever fears Him and works righteousness is accepted by Him [already].
>
> *Acts 10:34-35*

God however wants everyone to be a partaker of all He offers. He wants all folk to know the whole truth; not just to be saved. This is why Paul says 'and to come to the knowledge of the truth'. He then lists the basic truth God desires all men to know.

> . . . [God] desires all men to be saved and to come to the knowledge of the truth. For *there is* one God and one Mediator between God and men, *the* Man Christ Jesus, who gave Himself a ransom for all . . .
>
> *1 Timothy 2:4-6*

Basically, God wants all those in such a position to become a full part of His body, The Church. The benefits of this are numerous. Not least will be a more fruitful understanding and knowledge of God in Person and His ways. Coupled with that, there is the Person and empowering of the Holy Spirit.

All this and more enables a new life now capable of direct intervention against the powers of darkness.

The direct guidance and leading of God is accessible to the life of a Christian by the 'gifts of the Spirit' in a body of believers, as mentioned in 1 Corinthians 12 for example.

The removal of any fear of death and the 'beyond' is realistic. All in all it clearly makes the person a full part of the kingdom of God.

But probably the greatest benefit is assurance of salvation out of a living relationship with the living God. Certainly it is the best one to show the need to evangelise them.

The Wicked

The wicked as shown in chapter 9 have a fearful destiny. God has no pleasure in them going into such a future.

Now if we are His children our heart should be renewed with His love for Man, and that includes the wicked. For when you are related to someone and love them deeply, you identify naturally with their feelings. God paid the highest price to enable all who would to be free.

Free from sin and its power, as well as free from the power of Satan and His lies, thus free to get off the road to such a destiny. So God's feelings are apparent. The need for sharing the gospel with the wicked is clear. It is God's desire and ours if we are His. It is good news for those who recognise their need, and our task involves helping them to recognise this need.

On top of all this feeling and desire to share such news, such information about spiritual things, the Lord actually commands us to witness to it. If we are his disciples then there is little option to do otherwise, that is to say, irrespective of our feelings as mentioned. If we already desire to do this, however, it is not a duty but a delight. If we are becoming more like Jesus then our feelings of care and concern will naturally grow more like his.

What is this command? In the last paragraph in Matthew's gospel Jesus says to his disciples:

> . . . All authority has been given to Me in heaven and on earth. Go therefore and make disciples of all the nations, baptising them in the name of the Father and of the Son and of the Holy Spirit, teaching them to observe all things that I have commanded you;

> and lo, I am with you always, *even* to the end of the age . . . *Matthew 28:18-20*

The beauty about God is that He not only tells us what to do, but He also enables us to do it, teaching us, empowering us and putting His rubber stamp on our work. Just like a good employer who will not just give a task to his employee but also give him time to do it, the facilities, the know-how, in the measure of his limitations, etc. Once the task is complete, he will pass it on to another department putting his stamp of approval on the completed work.

We can see this in the above passage because the command to witness, or should I say to make disciples, is sandwiched in between the authority Jesus has and the knowledge and experience that Jesus had taught them. Making disciples is not a case of just telling people that God loves them and what He has done for them, it is a demonstration of His love in the life of the disciple sharing the news as well as the power and authority of God.

Such that this particular gospel cannot be said to have truly been fully heard by someone if all they have heard is a few words.

Have they seen sincerity in the life of the witness? Have they seen the power of God at work? Have they known the conviction from the Holy Spirit while they were listening?

This is part and parcel of the teaching and experiences Jesus gave to his disciples. They were taught to heal the sick, cast out demons, instruct on the kingdom, live a loving life etc. This is the context Jesus gave in which the gospel should be shared.

Even then, he did not say just tell them what I have done for them, e.g. Jesus died for you and rose again . . . He said to teach about the kingdom of God and all it entails, the whole counsel of God.

We need to teach people about things of God starting from where they are at; starting from their perspective, their standpoint of understanding. Jesus did this all the time: Whether it was a foreign woman at a well, an officer of the occupying army on a road, a blind man outside a building or other. He met them where they were at in their faith, in their understanding, in their misgivings, in their point of need . . .

God has put a measure of common sense and logic in all of us. There is a measure of right and wrong in all of us. Let us use these as our platforms from God in their lives, for which to launch our contacts, launch our evangelism in God's way, God's methods, by God's power.

Not forgetting, of course, the most important preparation Jesus gave his disciples, the spiritual angle on all this. He taught them to pray, to look at the Word afresh and to combat the enemy. This is the preparation of the ground prior to sowing.

Another Gospel

There is another gospel: the good news God has put

before all mankind as a witness to himself. It is His creation. By this witness alone we are told that Man has no excuse for not turning to God.

> . . . because what may be known of God is manifest in them, for God has shown *it* to them. For since the creation of the world his invisible *attributes* are clearly seen, being understood by the things that are made, *even* His eternal power and Godhead, so that they are without excuse . . . *Romans 1:19-20*

Paul goes on to say about this gospel, this good witness to God:

> . . . *Their sound has gone out to all the earth, and their words to the ends of the world.*
>
> *Romans 10:18*

This is a direct quote of Paul out of Psalm 19:4. The preceding verses read,

> The heavens declare the glory of God; and the firmament shows His handiwork. Day unto day utters speech, and night unto night reveals knowledge. *There is* no speech nor language *where* their voice is not heard. *Psalm 19:1-3*

In other words, God has not left himself without a witness. Creation is a testimony to His existence and reality. This alone is always a good foundation to build on in sharing the gospel of Jesus Christ.

Coupled to this, the understanding of God's fairness and just outlook as explained in the majority of this book and throughout scripture, there is a powerful argument to build on. The witness of Creation as well as that of the light of Jesus by his Spirit (as discussed), are revelation to every man alive. God wants his Church to add to this, their life and verbal testimony as a final witness to himself. This is the context of our sharing the gospel of Jesus Christ.

God's Purpose

God's reason for such an array, such a type of witness is to continue the genuine freedom of choice to everyone.

God has not made any automatons. Having said that, His angels never had any choice not to believe: They could see God at first hand: Any of them therefore who rebel are instantly without excuse (absolutely). This makes their kind of choice absolute.

Man was made with freedom to decide. God desires us to choose for Him. If He made it so obvious to all men that He is, it would no longer be a decision on our part out of a desire for the things of God, but this would instead be imposed on us to believe. This is not what God wants, indeed it is in His power to reveal himself to everyone in an instant, but it is not in His nature to do so. He is gentle and loving and wants us to desire these things for ourselves. His purpose is that His relationship with us is genuine, not automatic, but alive: A living choice, not like robots.

He therefore does not want us to impose Him on others but instead draw people to Him, to build upon the witness He has started. Let us take on this nature of God. Let us see His purposes. Let us work with Him and not against Him in all of this. Let us work together to teach, to reveal Him as He is, His way.

What now?

We cannot deny this? The above explanations in this book show the hope as a reality for many who have not heard of Jesus. Should we deny these also the knowledge of the One who paid for all this?

I believe as Christians when we begin to see that the Lord has a bigger heart and accepts many more people than we first believed we will be transformed into an accepting and more loving Church. We will become more approachable and a better light to all these who need to hear about the One they are trying to follow. Many more will be drawn to Jesus because of the new love realised by this truth.

We need to share that the One, they 'are believing in': His character, came down and died by shedding His blood on a cross for them. His love has made a way for a full relationship with Him as His adopted sons. His is the full and final substitute: His death instead of ours so we can have His Life now.

How does one become a Christian?

Having explained an understanding of who believes in the name of the Son of God as a believer in righteousness John 3:16 as a text makes even more sense.

> For God so loved the world that He gave His only begotten Son, that whoever believes in Him should not perish but have everlasting life. *John 3:16*

We saw how in New Testament Greek the verb 'to believe' here is in a tense known as the Present Active (I mentioned it as 'present continuous'). So, whoever 'is believing' in Him refers in context to those who are born again: Those who believe in the name of the Son of God: Believers in righteousness as testified by their practise of righteousness.

> . . . everyone who practises righteousness is born of Him. *1 John 2:29*

Jesus, God's only begotten Son was given by God out of his love. His death on a cross in our place enables us to have everlasting life. So now that you know about this sacrifice made for you here is a prayer which can help those who desire righteousness to enter fully. To begin a new phase to their journey: a conscious walk with the God who paid for their salvation:

> Dear God,
>
> Thank You for sending Jesus to pay the price for my salvation.

> I am sorry and I turn from all wrong I have done or am a part of.
>
> Thank You for Your love for me which has made this possible.
>
> I want to become a full part of Your Family and become Your child.
>
> I ask that You come into my life to make this a reality.
>
> I thank You in Jesus' name.
>
> Amen

Just as you have started praying, go on to talk with God.

Share with Him what you feel, and tell Him your cares, for He cares for you (1 Peter 5:7; Matthew 6:9-15; Matthew 11:28-30). Ask Him to help you find fellow believers with whom you can share fellowship. Be encouraged to go on reading about Him in His book: the Bible. There you will also read about the Baptism in the Holy Spirit which will enable you to be an effective witness and have more of God in your life.

(I have written a separate article about this entitled *What is Baptism in the Holy Spirit?* And can be read at www.jarom.net)

Go on being filled with His Spirit for that is the Life that enables our transformation into full and mature sons of God (Ephesians 5:18-19; Romans 12:1-2).

As you do all this, your Journey into Light will get brighter and brighter and you will walk as a child of light (2 Corinthians 3:18 & Ephesians 5:8).

12

CONCLUSION

Will there be Non-Christians in heaven?

Before Jesus Christ was born, men and women died as servants of God in the nation of Israel and elsewhere. They were followers of God and will go on to live in His presence. So already we know that there will be 'non-Christians' in heaven.

There is no evidence in the Bible that God treats people differently whether they existed before or after Jesus came. If this were so, there would be a cut-off point somewhere; there is no witness to such.

The witness we have in the Bible, as to what happens, is that of justice carried out according to the testimony received about God. This testimony improved dramatically with Jesus but it is only relevant to those who hear it. Judgment is directly given in accordance with what is known, what has been revealed.

One of the first witnesses is probably God's creation, then came the law as it was given to the people of Israel, then came Jesus. But throughout time Jesus reveals himself by His Spirit as light to all to turn to (John 1:9).

Such that (without confusing the use of the name Christian), it can be said people have turned to Christ and will be in heaven with Him without having heard of his death on the cross for them. Without consciously knowing it is Jesus they have been following until they see Him. Not unlike the faithful Jews who will be alive at Jesus' second coming who will recognise Him for the first time as their God and Messiah (Zechariah 12:10-11).

I have explained the value and importance as Christian believers to evangelise those in such a position, those whom the Bible also calls 'The Righteous'.

'The Wicked' are all those who have up till now turned their back on the light revealed to them, as testified to by their practise of wickedness, their life of evil.

This then leaves us with a challenge. If we are believers, the challenge is to encourage others to sow in their lives the kind of things they really want to reap.

> Do not be deceived, God is not mocked [fooled]; for whatever a man sows, that he will also reap. For he who sows to his flesh will of the flesh reap corruption, but he who sows to the Spirit will of the Spirit reap everlasting life. And let us not grow weary while doing good, for in due season we shall reap if we do not lose heart. *Galatians 6:7-9*

Sowing to the Spirit is the activity the righteous are involved in. They will reap everlasting life and it is a blessing for them to encourage others to do likewise.

> The fruit of the righteous *is a* tree of life, and he who wins souls *is* wise. *Proverbs 11:30*

Indeed,

> In the way of righteousness *is* life, and in *its* pathway *there is* no death. *Proverbs 12:28*

> The way of the wicked *is* an abomination to the LORD, but He loves him who follows righteousness. *Proverbs 15:9*

See also Proverbs 21:21, 11:20, 14:2 and 22, 14:31-32 etc. I have discussed how the context of scripture shows that the heart of the faith within, as producers of righteous deeds is accounted worthy and is acceptable to God. God looks at the blood of Jesus which he shed as the fulfilment, the substitute for all: those He wants and who wants: As clearly revealed by their deeds which are a natural fruit of the faith in their heart. It is this faith that God recognises. This is not because they have not sinned at all. It is not because they are faultless in their daily life. It is because what they know to be wrong is not desired by them and they, out of this heart of faith refuse to do it. God, by His grace will impart salvation to them. For,

> Blessed *are* those who hunger and thirst for righteousness, for they shall be filled. *Matthew 5:6*

Finally

I believe that showing the heart of God as it is will prove a powerful attraction to Him. Explaining how just and fair God is will appeal to the sense of morality of many and thus be a very powerful magnet for them to respond to. Not forgetting the equal attraction of knowing about His love, His amazing love which meant that He was willing to give His life by the shedding of His blood for us.

> . . . He *was* wounded for our transgressions, *He was* bruised for our iniquities; the chastisement for our peace *was* upon Him . . .
>
> . . . And the LORD has laid on Him the iniquity of us all. *Isaiah 53:5, 6*

What a Love! I believe this coupled with the understanding of how just and fair God really is, will lead to many thousands and thousands (millions?) to come to know Jesus.

LIST OF BIBLE PASSAGES USED

ACTS

ROMANS

1 Corinthians

2 Corinthians

Galatians

Ephesians

1 John

Jude

Revelation

Santo marcho

Una convergenza che si sarebbe realizzata proprio sul piano politico, ma anche su quello religioso. L'appoggio che Cosimo il 'Vecchio' non aveva mai fatto mancare al movimento dell'Osservanza domenicana, cui faceva capo anche il convento di San Marco e quindi lo stesso Savonarola, fu ereditato da Lorenzo sempre con l'intenzione di rafforzare la posizione della casa medícea nella Chiesa fiorentina a spese della fazione degli oligarchi. Per tutto il periodo che va dal 1434 al 1494 i Medici continuarono a investire risorse nel convento di San Marco. Per esempio, promuovendo già alla fine degli anni '80 del Quattrocento la canonizzazione di Antonino Pierozzi, frate domenicano dell'Osservanza e vescovo di Firenze, personaggio molto popolare a Firenze, la cui vicenda viene vivacemente illustrata dagli affreschi del primo chiostro che oggi il visitatore incontra entrando nell'ex-convento di San Marco.

Nel 1489 Lorenzo anticipò addirittura le istanze, espresse più tardi anche dal Savonarola, di separare la comunità di San Marco dalla Congregazione lombarda per ottenere maggiore autonomia nell'iniziativa riformatrice e garanzie di non dover abbandonare improvvisamente l'opera intrapresa.

In quello stesso anno entrarono nel convento due membri della famiglia dei Medici e nei dieci anni successivi saranno non meno di cinque i Medici presenti nella popolazione del convento. In quegli anni, dunque, il priore di San Marco era consapevole che l'opportunità di effettuare il suo programma religioso dipendesse in larga misura dalla parte medícea e non da quella a lei avversa.

Anche sotto un altro aspetto il 'principe' di Firenze e Savonarola erano più vicini di quanto li abbiano descritti. Nel periodo

A concurrence that would have found expression not just on the political plane, but also on the religious one. The support that Cosimo the "Elder" had never failed to give to the movement of the Dominican Observance, to which the convent of San Marco and therefore Savonarola himself adhered, was continued by Lorenzo, with the same intention of strengthening the position of the Medici family in the Florentine Church at the expense of the faction of oligarchs. For the whole of the period from 1434 to 1494 the Medici went on investing resources in the convent of San Marco. For example, by promoting the canonization of Antonino Pierozzi as early as the end of the 1480s. Dominican friar of the Observance and bishop of Florence, Antonino was a very popular figure in the city whose story is illustrated in lively fashion by the frescoes of the first cloister that the visitor encounters today on entering the former convent of San Marco.

In 1489 Lorenzo even anticipated the requests, later put forward by Savonarola as well, to have the community of San Marco separated from the Lombard Congregation in order to obtain greater autonomy in the initiative of reform, as well as guarantees that the work undertaken would not have to be abandoned unexpectedly.

That same year two members of the Medici family entered the convent, and over the following ten years there would be no less than five Medici among the monks. So in that period the prior of San Marco must have been aware that the possibility of putting his religious program into effect depended to a large extent on the Medicean party and not on the one opposed to it.

There was another way in which the "prince" of Florence and Savonarola were closer than they have been painted. In the period from 1490 to 1492 the men of letters in Lorenzo's circle, Giovanni Pico,

Predica del Savonarola, xilografia in G. Savonarola, *Prediche sopra il Salmo "Quod Bonus Israel Deus"*, 1539.

Savonarola Preaching, *woodcut in G. Savonarola, Prediche sopra il Salmo "Quod Bonus Israel Deus," 1539.*

che va dal 1490 al 1492 i letterati della cerchia di Lorenzo, Giovanni Pico, Poliziano, i fratelli Benivieni, Giovanni Nesi, erano anche i seguaci più in vista del frate ferrarese.

Dopo la morte del 'Magnifico' i rapporti con la famiglia dei Medici si mantennero buoni almeno fino al settembre del 1494, allorché Savonarola vide nella discesa in Italia del re di Francia Carlo VIII di Valois l'adempiersi delle proprie visioni profetiche.

Dopo la cacciata di Piero – seppur in modo strumentale, ma come abbiamo visto non lontano dal vero –, la persona di Savonarola veniva tuttavia ancora associata alla fazione medicea. Lo si accusò infatti di tenere contatti con Piero in esilio, di proteggere i partigiani più compromessi con il vecchio regime, e anche di custodire nei sotterranei di San Marco i tesori dei Medici in attesa del loro ritorno a Firenze.

Solo il fallimento del tentativo di alcuni partigiani medícei di riportare Piero a

Politian, the Benivieni brothers and Giovanni Nesi, were also the most prominent followers of the friar from Ferrara.

After the death of the "Magnificent" his relations with the Medici family remained good at least up until the September of 1494, when Savonarola saw the invasion of Italy by the king of France, Charles VIII of Valois, as the fulfillment of his prophetic visions.

Even after the expulsion of Piero the figure of Savonarola was still associated with the Medici faction, and while the link was made for political reasons, we have seen that it was not far from the truth. In fact he was accused of maintaining contact with Piero in exile, of protecting those most compromised by their ties with the old regime and even of storing the treasures of the Medici in the vaults of San Marco in expectation of their return to Florence.

Only the failure of the attempt by some supporters of the Medici to bring Piero back to Florence brought about a real

Firenze segnò di fatto la frattura fra Savonarola e gli esponenti del vecchio regime da cui fu praticamente costretto a prendere le distanze. Una frattura che si concretizzò nelle parole del *Trattato circa il reggimento e governo della città di Firenze* del 1498, dove – per la prima volta – si parlava della divisione fra il Regno di Dio, espresso dal governo popolare, e il Regno del male, espresso dalla tirannide dei Medici.

Da qui partì quel processo di revisione storica che, comunque, portò anche all'elaborazione di un progetto politico alternativo a quello proposto dai Medici e dai loro alleati, e che sostenne l'idea della formazione di una Repubblica fiorentina, almeno fino al 1540.

Tornando a seguire il corso degli eventi nel loro svolgimento cronologico, troviamo nel maggio o, al più tardi, nel giugno del **1490** Girolamo Savonarola di nuovo a Firenze, dove dal 1° di agosto iniziò a predicare nella chiesa del convento di San Marco.

Come argomento centrale per un lungo ciclo di predicazione (più di cinque mesi) la scelta cadde sul Libro dell'Apocalisse. Per la prima volta a Firenze risuonarono le esortazioni già sentite a San Gimignano circa il prepararsi in fretta a fare penitenza. Stando al suo più antico biografo, la novità rispetto ai generici appelli alla penitenza, molto comuni in quegli anni da parte dei predicatori, fu che il frate di San Marco sosteneva apertamente che le sue affermazioni trovavano conferma nei passi delle Scritture, presentandosi di fatto come un profeta.

L'anno della sua elezione a priore di San Marco rimase memorabile anche per il fatto che durante la Quaresima del **1491** Savonarola predicò per la prima volta nella cattedrale.

break between Savonarola and the members of the old regime, from whom he was practically forced to dissociate himself. A rupture that found concrete expression in the words of the Trattato circa il reggimento e governo della città di Firenze *of 1498, where – for the first time – he spoke of the division between the Kingdom of God, represented by the popular government, and the Kingdom of Evil, symbolized by the tyranny of the Medici.*

This marked the beginning of a process of historical revision which, nevertheless, also led to the development of an alternative political program to the one proposed by the Medici and their allies, and which supported the idea of the formation of a Florentine republic, at least up until 1540.

Returning to the chronological sequence of events, in May or, at the latest, June of ***1490*** *we find Girolamo Savonarola back in Florence, where on August 1 he began to preach in the church of the convent of San Marco.*

As the central subject of a long series of sermons (lasting for over five months) his choice fell on the Book of Revelations. *For the first time the Florentines were exposed to the exhortations to make hasty preparations to do penance that had already been heard at San Gimignano.*

Going by his earliest biographer, the difference with respect to the generic appeals to penitence that were commonly made by preachers in those years lay in the fact that the friar of San Marco openly claimed that his assertions found confirmation in the Holy Scriptures, presenting himself de facto *as a prophet.*

The year of his appointment as prior of San Marco has also gone down in history for the fact that it was during Lent in **1491** *that Savonarola preached in the cathedral for the first time.*

Savonarola nello studio, xilografia del 1496.

Savonarola in His Study*, woodcut, 1496.*

La cella di Girolamo Savonarola nel Convento di San Marco, nell'allestimento del primo Novecento.

Girolamo Savonarola's cell in the monastery of San Marco, as it was fitted out in the early 20th century

L'attacco che Savonarola mosse in quel frangente alla strumentalizzazione della religione da parte del potere fu terribile, ma certo non si può arrivare a sostenere, come hanno fatto molti biografi, che la pietra dello scandalo fosse da individuare solo nella persona del 'Magnifico'.
Certo è che alla profezia Savonarola attribuisce anche una forte carica politica, nel senso che la ritiene capace di rilanciare quella 'religione' civica tipica dell'ambito comunale italiano, dove l'amore di Dio diventava amore nei confronti della comunità in cui si viveva, non solo cura di anime, ma anche cura dei corpi dei cittadini. Una religione cittadina che nella società fiorentina quattrocentesca si mostrava appagata nei suoi riti religiosi collettivi, nelle grandi processioni che esaltavano il potere di alcuni individui e di alcune famiglie.
È comprensibile che quando, poco tempo dopo, il frate agostiniano Mariano da Genazzano – predicando nel convento di San Gallo – incentrò il suo discorso sulle parole degli Atti degli Apostoli: «non sta a voi conoscere né il tempo né il momento», la sua predica fosse interpretata da molti fiorentini come la replica alle accuse di Savonarola da parte di un ambiente molto vicino al potere.
Il **1492** è segnato da tre avvenimenti che anche tradizionalmente sono considerati eventi chiave nella vicenda di Girolamo Savonarola.
Ai primi di aprile di quell'anno muore nella villa di Careggi Lorenzo dei Medici.
Veniva meno se non – come è stato detto con qualche esagerazione – 'l'ago della bilancia' della politica italiana, sicuramente un saldo punto di riferimento nella politica cittadina.
Due giorni prima Savonarola aveva evocato, dopo una lunga notte di riflessione, un'immagine che, come dimostra il suo

The attack that Savonarola launched on the exploitation of religion by those in power on that occasion was a fearsome one, but it is certainly not possible to argue, as many of his biographers have done, that the cause of all the trouble could be identified as Lorenzo the Magnificent.
What we do know is that Savonarola assigned a strong political role to prophecy as well, in the sense that he considered it capable of reviving the civic "religion" typical of the Italian communes, where the love of God became love for the community in which one lived: not just cure of souls, but also cure of the bodies of citizens. A civic religion that in 15th-century Florentine society found fulfillment in its collective religious rituals, in the great processions that exalted the power of certain individuals and certain families.
It is comprehensible that when, a short time later, the Augustinian friar Mariano da Genazzano – preaching in the convent of San Gallo – centered his sermon on the passage in the Acts of the Apostles in which Luke declares "It is not for you to know the times or the seasons," his words were interpreted by many Florentines as a response to Savonarola's accusations on the part of circles very close to those in power.
*The year **1492** was marked by three developments that are also traditionally considered key events in the life of Girolamo Savonarola. At the beginning of April of that year Lorenzo de' Medici died in the villa of Careggi. The man who, while he may not have "held the balance" of Italian politics as has been claimed with some exaggeration, was certainly a firm point of reference in the politics of the city had gone.*
Two days earlier, after a long night of reflection, Savonarola had conjured up an image that, as its extensive use in iconography demonstrates, was to leave a deep impres-

Savonarola benedice un gruppo di monache, xilografia in G. Savonarola, *Operetta molto divota...*, fine del sec. XV. Firenze, Biblioteca Nazionale Centrale.

Savonarola Blessing a Group of Nuns, *woodcut in G. Savonarola,* Operetta molto divota..., *late 15th cent. Biblioteca Nazionale Centrale, Florence.*

ampio uso iconografico, rimarrà ben scolpita nella mente dei suoi contemporanei. È quella famosa frase dal sapore profetico: «Ecco la spada di Dio sopra la terra tra breve e con rapidità», pronunciata durante una predica sul passo del Vangelo relativo a Lazzaro.

L'11 agosto, infine, sale sul soglio di Pietro Alessandro VI che, come vedremo, contribuirà con la sua politica a rendere più fragile la posizione del priore di San Marco nelle turbolente vicende cittadine alla fine del decennio. Ma intanto tutto sembra andare per il meglio per il frate e i suoi seguaci.

Infatti, l'anno successivo (**1493**) la popolarità di Savonarola è ormai diventata così grande da attirare al convento di San Marco molti novizi – la popolazione del convento sale a più di 90 frati –, lasciti e

sion on the mind of his contemporaries. It was that famous phrase of prophetic flavor – "The sword of God upon the earth, swift and sudden!" –pronounced during a sermon on the Gospel story of Lazarus.

Finally, on August 11, Alexander VI ascended Peter's throne: as we shall see, the pope's policy would contribute to the weakening of the prior of San Marco's position in the upheavals through which the city passed at the end of the decade. In the meantime, however, all seemed to be going well for the friar and his disciples.

*By the following year (**1493**), in fact, Savonarola's popularity had grown so great that many new novices were attracted to the convent of San Marco (the number of monks in the monastery rose to over ninety), along with bequests and donations. In*

Antonio Capecchi, *Savonarola invita Carlo VIII ad abbandonare Firenze*, 1853. Firenze, Palazzo Vecchio.

Antonio Capecchi, Savonarola Inviting Charles VIII to Leave Florence, *1853. Palazzo Vecchio, Florence.*

donazioni. Di comune accordo con Piero dei Medici, suo fratello il cardinale Giovanni (futuro papa Leone X) e con la benedizione del cardinale protettore dell'Ordine Oliviero Caraffa, il priore del convento di San Marco fra' Girolamo Savonarola e i suoi confratelli inoltrano nel maggio di quell'anno una richiesta formale al Papa per ottenere l'autonomia dalla Congregazione di Lombardia.
Il convento di San Marco, nelle intenzioni del suo priore ma anche del governo cittadino, dovrebbe diventare il centro di una provincia autonoma che includa tutti i conventi dell'Osservanza domenicana in Toscana. L'obiettivo sembra raggiunto nel novembre quando il generale dell'Ordine dona a Savonarola i poteri di padre provinciale e pone sotto la cura spirituale del priore di San Marco i conventi di Fiesole, Pisa e San Gimignano.

May of that year, with the consent of Piero de' Medici and his brother Cardinal Giovanni (the future Pope Leo X) and the blessing of the cardinal protector of the order Oliviero Caraffa, the prior of the convent of San Marco Fra Girolamo Savonarola and his fellow monks sent a formal request to the pope asking to be granted autonomy from the Congregation of Lombardy.
The convent of San Marco, in the intentions not only of its prior but of the city government too, was to become the center of an independent province that would include all the monasteries of the Dominican Observance in Tuscany. Their goal seemed to have been attained in November when the general of the order assigned Savonarola the powers of provincial and placed the monasteries of Fiesole, Pisa and San Gimignano under the spiritual care of the prior of San Marco.

Savonarola fra la Repubblica e il Papato

Lo stato delle cose muta improvvisamente nel **1494** e si evolve in una direzione contraria alle speranze del predicatore domenicano di rendere Firenze il centro di un movimento riformatore che si sarebbe propagato in tutta la penisola. Condizione essenziale alla riforma era la pace e proprio quest'ultima in breve venne meno.

All'inizio di quell'anno muore Ferdinando d'Aragona (detto Ferrante) re di Napoli. Carlo VIII re di Francia, alleatosi con Ludovico Sforza (meglio conosciuto come 'il Moro') duca di Milano, prepara la sua discesa in Italia per appropriarsi del Regno di Napoli. Il 4 di ottobre Piero abbandona Firenze, dopo aver consegnato a Carlo le fortezze di Sarzana e Pietrasanta e dopo aver assicurato al re l'accesso alla città di Pisa e al porto di Livorno.

Nei mesi successivi Savonarola spende tutta la sua energia per spronare i fiorentini a edificare lo 'Stato Nuovo'. Un'energia quantificabile nelle ventitré prediche *Sopra Aggeo*, il cui senso verrà da lui stesso riepilogato nella II delle prediche sui *Salmi* nel gennaio del '95: «Io ti ho detto quattro cose [Firenze] se non le farai guai a te: prima il timore di Dio, secundo il bene comune; terzio la pace universale; quarto la riforma [dello Stato]. Voi avete cominciato a rovescio, cioè dalla riforma che era l'ultima. Seguitate almeno a rovescio e fate questa pace, che se non la fate sarà la ruina vostra».

Il 24 dicembre, infatti, era stata approvata dal governo provvisorio della Repubblica la nascita di un Consiglio Grande, un vero organo di governo che doveva garantire l'allargamento della partecipazione po-

Savonarola between the Republic and the Papacy

There was an unexpected change in the situation in ***1494*** *and things began to move in a direction that went against the Dominican preacher's hopes of making Florence the center of a movement of reform that would spread throughout the peninsula. An essential condition for reform was peace and that is precisely what was about to disappear.*

At the beginning of that year the king of Naples, Ferdinand of Aragon (called Ferrante), died. King Charles VIII of France, in alliance with Ludovico Sforza (better known as "il Moro'), duke of Milan, prepared to invade Italy in order to seize the kingdom of Naples. On October 4, Piero fled from Florence, after handing over the fortresses of Sarzana and Pietrasanta to Charles and guaranteeing him access to the city of Pisa and the port of Livorno.

Over the following months Savonarola devoted all his energy to urging the Florentines to build the "New State." Energy that was channeled into the twenty-three sermons Sopra Aggeo *("On Haggai"), whose message would be summed in the second of his sermons on the* Psalms *in January 1495: "I have told you [Florence] four things. Woe betide you if you do not do them: first the fear of God, second the commonwealth; third universal peace; fourth reform [of the State]. You have begun them back to front, that is from reform which was the last. At least carry on backward and make this peace, which if you do not will be your ruin."*

On December 24, in fact, the provisional government of the republic had approved the setting up of a Grand Council, a true organ of government that was to guarantee the broadening of popular participa-

polare e per le cui adunanze fu costruita una nuova sede nel palazzo della Signoria: il Salone dei Cinquecento. Esso è l'arca che, nelle prediche ai *Salmi* – ventinove prediche che coprono buona parte del 1495 –, Savonarola incalza i fiorentini a costruire anche a costo di ritardare i lavori alla fabbrica della cattedrale; il segno tangibile che il disegno divino si sta realizzando.

Se, dunque, è improprio parlare dell'affermarsi fra il '94 e il '98 di una "repubblica savonaroliana", è invece proprio questa funzione di sprone allo smantellamento del vecchio assetto di potere che la moderna storiografia riconosce in modo unanime al frate ferrarese.

Inizia però in quell'anno anche il delinearsi di una fazione contraria alle ingerenze del frate nella politica cittadina. Il suo biografo più attendibile, Roberto Ridolfi, ritiene di poter attribuire la pianificazione di un vero e proprio complotto, che ebbe come protagonisti il Gonfaloniere di Giustizia Filippo Corbizzi, il priore di Santa Maria Novella e il frate francescano Domenico da Ponzo, al giudizio negativo più volte espresso da Savonarola nei confronti della cosiddetta legge "delle sei fave", in base alla quale con soli sei voti la Signoria poteva "tirannicamente" – per usare un aggettivo caro al nostro frate – disporre a suo piacere della vita e dei beni dei cittadini.

Una pubblica disputa fra Savonarola e il Minore si tenne effettivamente nel palazzo della Signoria; una disputa nel corso della quale Savonarola seppe respingere gli attacchi di chi lo accusava di intromettersi indebitamente nella politica cittadina, portando a esempio le vite di santi come san Pietro Martire e santa Caterina da Siena e l'opera svolta dal cardinale Giovanni Latino, anch'egli do-

tion. A new seat for its assemblies was created in the Palazzo della Signoria: the Salone del Cinquecento. It was the arch that, in his sermons on the Psalms *(twenty-nine of them, covering much of 1495), Savonarola pressed the Florentines to build even at the cost of delaying work on the cathedral: a tangible sign that the divine plan was being fulfilled.*

So while it is inaccurate to speak of the establishment of a "Savonarolan republic" between 1494 and 1498, it is this function of a spur to the dismantling of the old power structure that modern historians unanimously assign to the Ferrarese friar.

But that year also saw the emergence of a faction opposed to the friar's meddling in the city's politics. His most reliable biographer, Roberto Ridolfi, claimed that the hatching of a genuine plot, involving the Gonfalonier of Justice Filippo Corbizzi, the prior of Santa Maria Novella and the Franciscan friar Domenico da Ponzo, could be blamed on the negative view expressed by Savonarola several times with regard to the so-called law of the "six beans." This was a reference to the fact that the city's supreme executive council, the Signoria, was able to "tyrannically" (an adjective of which the friar was fond) do as it willed with the life and property of citizens on the basis of just six votes.

A public debate was actually held between Savonarola and the Friar Minor in the Palazzo della Signoria: Savonarola used the debate as an opportunity to repulse the attacks of those who accused him of unwanted interference in the city's politics, offering as an example the lives of saints like Peter Martyr and Catherine of Siena and the efforts made by Cardinal Giovanni Latino, another Dominican, to settle the conflicts be-

Savonarola offre il trattato alla Badessa del convento delle Murate, xilografia in G. Savonarola, *Operetta molto divota...*, fine del sec. XV. Firenze, Biblioteca Nazionale Centrale.

Savonarola Offering His Treatise to the Abbess of the Convent of the Murate, *woodcut in G. Savonarola,* Operetta molto divota..., *late 15th cent. Biblioteca Nazionale Centrale, Florence.*

menicano, nel comporre i dissidi che vi furono un tempo in Firenze fra Guelfi e Ghibellini.
Nel frattempo l'avventura di Carlo VIII in Italia volgeva ormai al termine.
In un breve lasso di tempo, infatti, si erano coalizzati contro di lui per combatterlo il suo ex alleato Ludovico Sforza, la Repubblica veneta, l'imperatore e il re di Spagna.
Era nata così una 'Lega' che aveva avuto la benedizione del Papa. Il 6 di luglio a Fornovo le sue schiere affrontarono le truppe di Carlo che stava risalendo la penisola e le sconfissero, costringendo Carlo a una precipitosa ritirata al di là delle Alpi.
La Repubblica fiorentina era rimasta neutrale nel conflitto e fu facile credere o essere indotti a credere che il governo di Firenze

tween Guelphs and Ghibellines that had once riven Florence.
In the meantime Charles VIII's adventure in Italy was drawing to a close.
Within a short space of time, in fact, he found himself facing a coalition of his former ally Ludovico Sforza, the Venetian Republic, the emperor and the king of Spain.
Thus a "Holy League" was created that had the blessing of the pope. At Fornovo on July 6 its forces confronted Charles's troops, which were making their way back up the peninsula, and defeated them, obliging Charles to beat a hasty retreat across the Alps.
The Florentine Republic had remained neutral in the conflict and it was easy to believe or to be led to believe that the

Santa maria delfiore

ostrasi inque
one misure
fezione ede
fonti dellan
io apiezan
ezito
si dimostra
elo enelm
torre. sol
do. Rano
ficzati:—
E bij
dets
ja bra. 160.
una clare
lez. navi
160.
laltezza d
a difuori
taluns
ta due. tal
a chiesa. si
E dall
amp
eduta n
ondiuo
etarsie
q. ½. lurio
ofeij. 16. E
delle mar
mo ditutte

¶ COMPENDIO DI REVELATIONE DELLO INVTILE SERVO DI IESV CHRISTO FRATE HIERONYMO DA FERRA RA DELLORDINE DE FRA TI PREDICATORI

¶ IESVS MARIA

BENCHE Lungo tempo in molti modi per inſpiratione Diuina io habbia predecte mol te choſe future: nientedimeno conſiderando laſententia del noſtro ſaluatore chriſto Ieſu che dice. Nolite ſanctum dare canibus: nec mittatis mar garitas ueſtras ante porcos: ne forte conculcent eas pedi bus: & cõuerſi dirumpant uos: Sono ſempre ſtato ſcarſo nel dire: & non miſono exteſo piu che miſia parſo eſſere neceſſario alla ſalute degli huomini / in modo che le con cluſione noſtre ſono ſtate poche/ aduengha che molte ſie

Savonarola predica nel Duomo di Firenze, xilografia in G. Savonarola, *Compendio di Revelatione*, 1496. Firenze, Biblioteca Nazionale Centrale.

Savonarola Preaching in Florence Cathedral, *woodcut in G. Savonarola,* Compendio di Revelatione, *1496. Biblioteca Nazionale Centrale, Florence.*

Nella pagina accanto:
Marco di Bartolomeo Rustici, *Santa Maria del Fiore*, 1447-48. Firenze, Biblioteca del Seminario Maggiore del Cestello.

Facing page:
Marco di Bartolomeo Rustici, Santa Maria del Fiore, *1447-48. Biblioteca del Seminario Maggiore del Cestello, Florence.*

L'Adorazione del Crocefisso con Gerusalemme, Roma e Firenze sullo sfondo, xilografia del 1496 che rappresenta la visione avuta dal Savonarola nella notte del Venerdì Santo dello stesso anno.

Adoration of Christ Crucified with Jerusalem, Rome and Florence in the Background, *woodcut of 1496 representing the vision Savonarola had on the eve of Good Friday of the same year.*

seguisse alla lettera le indicazioni politiche che gli venivano dal priore di San Marco. Del resto Savonarola nel suo ultimo ciclo di prediche, quelle dette sopra i *Salmi*, aveva sostenuto che Firenze non doveva «far lega se non con Cristo» e facendo continuamente riferimento a una «riforma della Chiesa» poteva realmente essere scambiato per il fautore di una politica filo-francese.

Di qui l'ingiunzione al silenzio fatta pervenire da Alessandro VI al Savonarola attraverso due Brevi (circolari con il sigillo papale), uno datato all'8 settembre, l'altro al 16 ottobre del **1495**, probabilmente suggerita da chi a Firenze vedeva di buon occhio un'alleanza con la 'Lega'.

Fu in questa occasione che il frate predicatore si mostrò particolarmente attento alle potenzialità della stampa a caratteri mobili nel raggiungere un vasto pubblico in pochissimo tempo e mandò ai torchi un breve scritto apologetico, intitolandolo *Epistola a un amico*.

In essa il Savonarola conferma minutamente le sue posizioni e porta a testimone, per mezzo di quella stampa, la stampa delle altre sue opere per far notare che da esse non è mai emerso niente che gli si potesse rimproverare.

Contemporaneamente, anche la Signoria cercò di perorare la causa del suo cittadino presso il Pontefice.

Dopo aver cercato di assicurare il priore di San Marco alla tutela della neonata Congregazione tosco-romana, e quindi del suo fiero avversario Francesco Mei che ne era stato nominato 'reggitore' – una subordinazione cui si opposero con grande forza i frati del convento fiorentino e che perciò rimase lettera morta –, nel febbraio del **1496** il Papa consentì a Savonarola di riprendere la predicazione.

Iniziò dunque quel ciclo di prediche, dette "Sopra Amos", in cui Savonarola conti-

government of Florence was following the political instructions of the prior of San Marco to the letter. Moreover in his last cycle of sermons, the ones on the Psalms, *Savonarola had argued that Florence should not "ally itself with anyone but Christ" and, with his continual references to "reform of the Church," could really have been mistaken for the supporter of a pro-French policy.*

Whence the injunction to silence that Alexander VI sent to Savonarola by means of two briefs (letters with the papal seal), one dated September 8, the other October 16, ***1495****, probably at the suggestion of someone in Florence who looked favorably on an alliance with the "League."*

On this occasion the friar preacher showed that he was well aware of the ability of movable-type printing to reach a large proportion of the public in a very short time and sent a short apologetic text to the presses, entitling it Epistola a un amico *("Letter to a Friend").*

Savonarola confirmed his positions in detail in this printed text, and called to witness the printed versions of his other works in order to show that he had never said anything in them for which he could be rebuked.

At the same time, the Signoria too sought to plead its citizen's cause with the pontiff.

After trying to place the prior of San Marco under the authority of the newly created Tusco-Roman Congregation, and thus of his fierce opponent Francesco Mei who had been appointed its "governor" (a subordination which the friars of the Florentine monastery resisted with great force and thus remained a dead letter), the pope allowed Savonarola to resume preaching in February ***1496****.*

And so Savonarola embarked on his series of sermons on Amos, in which he nuava a perseguire con tenacia il proprio intento riformatore.

Famosa è l'invettiva il cui *incipit* si rivolge direttamente ai suoi nemici che, come abbiamo visto, proprio in quell'anno brigavano con il papa Borgia: «Ne prophetetis! Essi non vogliono che si profeti. Dimmi perché vuoi scacciare questa Grazia dalla Chiesa?».

Il Savonarola è infatti fermamente convinto di essere depositario di una Grazia che sottrae lui e la sua opera a ogni giudizio umano. «Ogni volta dunque che si potesse vedere espressamente – continua – che li comandamenti delli superiori sono contrari alli comandamenti di Dio e massimamente al precetto di carità, niuno debbe obbedire in questo caso [...] quando io vedessi espressamente che il mio partire d'una città fusse ruina spirituale e corporale del popolo, non obedirìa a uomo vivente che mi comandassi che io mi partissi».

continued to pursue his reformist aims with tenacity.

*They include a famous tirade whose opening words were aimed directly at his enemies, engaged, as we have seen, in intrigues with the Borgia pope that very year: "*Ne prophetetis! *They do not want prophecy. Tell my why you wish to drive this Grace from the Church?"*

In fact Savonarola was firmly convinced that he had been entrusted with a Grace that placed him and his work above any human judgment. "Thus every time it can clearly be seen," he went on, "that the commandments of superiors are contrary to the commandments of God and especially to the precept of charity, no one should obey them [and] when I see clearly that my departure from a city would mean the spiritual and bodily ruin of its people, I will not obey any living man who should order me to leave."

La scomunica di fra' Girolamo e il supplizio

Uscito apparentemente vincitore dallo scontro con il Papa, il nostro frate iniziò in modo propizio anche l'anno successivo (**1497**), che sarà invece quello della scomunica.

A capo della Signoria era stato eletto come Gonfaloniere Francesco Valori, vero e proprio capo della fazione pro-Savonarola che veniva chiamata dai suoi avversari dei "Piagnoni".

Il 7 febbraio si tenne il "bruciamento delle vanità" che Savonarola volle inscenare nell'odierna piazza della Signoria; un rito che fu ripetuto l'anno successivo sempre durante il Carnevale.

Su una piramide di legno a gradini – forse sette per analogia con i peccati capitali, ma alcune fonti parlano di quindici – fu-

The Excommunication and Execution of Fra Girolamo

*After this apparent victory in his clash with the pope, the following year (**1497**) began in a propitious way for the friar, but was eventually to lead to his excommunication.*

The newly elected gonfalonier and head of the Signoria was Francesco Valori, leader of the pro-Savonarola faction that was called the "Piagnoni" by its adversaries.

On February 7 Savonarola staged the "bonfire of the vanities" in what is now Piazza della Signoria; a ritual that was repeated the following year, again at Carnival time.

On a pyramid of wooden steps – perhaps seven by analogy with the deadly sins, although some sources speak of fifteen – were placed objects representing the vices of the men and women of Florence:

Queſta cogitatione della mortelhanno hauuta tucti li ſancti
huomini &ſancte donne :& inogni opera che efanno tucta

La morte mostra a un giovane il cielo e l'inferno, xilografia in G. Savonarola, *Predica dell'arte del Bene morire*, 1496 ca. Firenze, Biblioteca Nazionale Centrale.

Death Showing a Young Man Heaven and Hell, *woodcut in G. Savonarola,* Predica dell'arte del Bene morire, *c. 1496. Biblioteca Nazionale Centrale, Florence.*

Ludwig von Langenmantel, Savonarola predica contro il lusso e prepara il "bruciamento delle vanità", particolare, 1881. Già Monaco, Galerie Kunstverein.

Ludwig von Langenmantel, Savonarola Preaching against Luxury and Preparing the "Bonfire of the Vanities", *detail, 1881. Formerly in the Galerie Kunstverein, Munich.*

rono collocati degli oggetti che rappresentavano i vizi delle donne e degli uomini di Firenze: dalle stoffe preziose alle scacchiere alle carte da giuoco, dagli strumenti musicali ai belletti e ai profumi fino ai libri e ai quadri.
Non si trattava certo di una novità. Già il francescano san Bernardino da Siena nel 1424 aveva organizzato proprio a Firenze, in piazza Santa Croce, un grande falò nel quale erano stati arsi oggetti ritenuti strumenti del diavolo, ma l'episodio fu un'altra occasione sfruttata dai detrattori del frate per attaccarlo. Fu infatti accusato di aver letteralmente mandato in fumo ventimila ducati di roba, la somma che, narrano le cronache, un mercante veneziano avrebbe offerto alla Signoria per l'insieme degli oggetti in attesa di essere bruciati.
Ma la situazione politica stava rapidamente e pericolosamente volgendo al peggio. Raggiunto un accordo fra la 'Lega' e il re

from precious fabrics to chessboards and playing cards, from musical instruments to cosmetics, perfumes and even books and pictures.
There was certainly nothing new in this. In 1424 the Franciscan St. Bernardine of Siena had organized a large bonfire in Florence, in Piazza Santa Croce, on which objects regarded as instruments of the devil had been burned. Yet the episode gave the friar's detractors another opportunity to attack him. In fact he was accused of having literally sent up in smoke twenty thousand ducats, the sum that, according to the chronicles, a Venetian merchant had offered to pay the Signoria for the objects waiting to be burned.
Politically, however, things were taking a rapid and dangerous turn for the worse. Following the reaching of an accord between the "League" and the king of France, who renounced his claims to the

Contra fratrem Hieronymum
Heresiarchā libellus et ꝓcessus.

Nosce teipm̄.
Qui potis es sathane versutos scire colubros
Tartareū impunis ire redire lacum.
Elysijs etiam dare tetra cadauera campis
Minheus/Ethereos ledere parce deos.
Non spinas pia Rhānus alit dū lilia gestit
Pontificem summū quisqꝫ beatus amat.

I diavoli ispirano il Savonarola. Xilografia in *Contra fratrem Hieronymum heresiarcham libellus et processus*, 1498 ca. Firenze, Biblioteca Nazionale Centrale.

Devils Inspiring Savonarola, *woodcut in* Contra fratrem Hieronymum heresiarcham libellus et processus, *c. 1498. Biblioteca Nazionale Centrale, Florence.*

Nelle pagine successive:
Francesco Rosselli (attr.), *Il supplizio di Girolamo Savonarola*, 1500 ca. Firenze, Museo di San Marco.

Following pages:
Francesco Rosselli (attrib.), The Execution of Girolamo Savonarola, *c. 1500. Museo di San Marco, Florence.*